잠언 쓰기를 시작하며 ✏️

잠언 쓰기를 시작한 이유와 쓰고 난 후 기대하는 점 등을 기록해 보세요.

시작한 날

년.   월.   일.

십대를 위한
잠언 **영어로** 한 달 쓰기
ESV®

일러두기

1. 성경 본문은 Crossway가 발행한 The Holy Bible, English Standard Version (ESV)을 사용했습니다.
2. '암송 구절 해설'은 《무디 성경 주석》(국제제자훈련원)의 내용을 토대로 작성했습니다.

십대를 위한
잠언 영어로 한 달 쓰기

사랑플러스 편집부 엮음

✤ 사랑플러스

잠언 쓰기,
세상을 지혜롭게 헤쳐 나갈 수 있는 힘

'나는 앞으로 무엇을 하면서 살아야 할까?'
'공부가 너무 힘들어. 어떻게 하면 잘할 수 있을까?'
'친구들이 나를 싫어하면 어쩌지?'
'부모님이 나 때문에 실망하시지는 않을까?'

답답하고 불안한 마음을 달래기 위해 스마트폰으로 친구들과 수다를 떨기도 하고, 코노(코인 노래방)에서 목청껏 노래도 해보고, 게임에 빠져들기도 하지만 좀처럼 마음을 다잡을 수 없습니다.

우리는 이렇게 고민되는 순간을 수없이 마주하며 살아갑니다. 그리고 매번 어려운 선택의 기로에 놓이기도 하지요. 하지만 그때마다 우리는 무엇이 옳은 선택인지, 내가 과연 잘하고 있는 것인지 헷갈리기만 합니다.

성경을 펼쳐 보아도 내 상황에 딱 맞는 말씀을 찾기란 쉽지 않아요. 성경 말씀은 '이럴 땐 이렇게 하고, 저럴 땐 저렇게 해야 한다'는 명확한 기준을 제시해 주는 것 같지 않거든요.

고민 많은 십대, 지혜가 필요해!

그렇다면 우리는 어떻게 중요한 일을 결정하고, 바른 선택을 할 수 있을까요? 그 해답은 바로 '지혜'에 있어요. 지혜는 바른 판단력과 분별력을 제공해 주는 가장 귀한 보물과 같습니다. 지혜로운 사람이 되면 하나님이 원하시는 것이 무엇인지, 나를 향한 계획은 무엇인지 찾을 수 있어요.

하지만 지혜가 없으면 자기도 모르게 죄에 빠질 수 있고, 심지어 하나님을 떠나기도 해요. 자, 그렇다면 이 지혜는 어떻게 얻을 수 있을까요? 성경의 '잠언'은 바로 그 지혜를 얻는 법을 알려 주는 책입니다.

지혜가 트이는 책, 잠언

잠언은 삶의 지혜를 짧은 문장들로 소개한 책이에요. 그래서 '지혜의 책'이라고도 불리지요. 잠언은 역사상 가장 지혜로운 사람이었던 이스라엘의 왕 솔로몬이 기록했어요. 솔로몬이 1장부터 31장까지 모두 쓴 것은 아니고 '지혜 있는 자'라고 불렸던 '아굴', '르무엘'도 저자로 등장하지요. 잠언은 대부분 궁정에서 쓰였지만, 내용을 보면 가정과 개인의 행실에 초점을 맞추어 우리가 실제로 어떻게 살아가야 하는지 상세하게 알려 주고 있어요. 따라서 우리는 잠언을 통해 '어떻게 사는 것이 잘 사는 인생'인지 명확하게 알 수 있지요.

읽는 걸론 부족해, 잠언 쓰기의 유익

여기서 한 가지 중요한 점! 읽기만 하면 되지 왜 굳이 써야 할까요? 귀찮기도 하고 시간도 없는데 말이에요. 한 글자, 한 글자 천천히 따라 쓰다 보면 생각하는 시간이 생기기 때문에 잠언의 말씀이 손과 머리 그리고 가슴 깊숙한 곳까지 뻗어 내려오는 걸 느낄 수 있어요. 중요한 말씀이 눈으로 슥 지나가지 않고 개념 하나하나가 생생하게 와닿는 경험을 할 수 있을 거예요. 뿐만 아니라 글을 잘 쓸 수 있는 능력이 생겨요. 좋은 문장을 따라 쓰면서 나도 모르는 사이에 어휘력과 문장력이 향상된답니다.

자, 이제 무궁무진한 지혜의 바다로 항해를 시작해 볼까요?

Proverbs 1

The Beginning of Knowledge

1   The proverbs of Solomon, son of David, king of Israel:

2   To know wisdom and instruction*, to understand words of insight,

3   to receive instruction in wise dealing, in righteousness, justice, and equity;

4   to give prudence to the simple**, knowledge and discretion to the youth—

5   Let the wise hear and increase in learning, and the one who understands obtain guidance,

6   to understand a proverb and a saying, the words of the wise and their riddles.

7   The fear of the LORD is the beginning of knowledge; fools despise wisdom and instruction.

The Enticement of Sinners

8   Hear, my son, your father's instruction, and forsake*** not your mother's teaching,

9   for they are a graceful garland for your head and pendants for your neck.

10 My son, if sinners entice you, do not consent.

---

*   instruction [instrʌ́kʃən] 똉 훈계, 교훈, 가르침, 훈련.

**   the simple 어리석은 자.

*** forsake [fərséik] 똉 떠나다, 그만두다, 포기하다.

11 If they say, "Come with us, let us lie in wait for blood; let us ambush* the innocent without reason;

12 like Sheol** let us swallow them alive, and whole, like those who go down to the pit;

13 we shall find all precious goods, we shall fill our houses with plunder;

14 throw in your lot among us; we will all have one purse"—

15 my son, do not walk in the way with them; hold back your foot from their paths,

16 for their feet run to evil, and they make haste to shed blood.

17 For in vain is a net spread in the sight of any bird,

18 but these men lie in wait for their own blood; they set an ambush for their own lives.

19 Such are the ways of everyone who is greedy for unjust gain; it takes away the life of its possessors.

*   ambush [æmbuʃ] ⑲ 매복, 잠복 ⑤ 매복하다.
**   Sheol [ʃiːoul] ⑲ (히브리 사람들의) 저승, 황천, 무덤, 지옥.

The Call of Wisdom

20 Wisdom cries aloud in the street, in the markets she raises her voice;

21 at the head of the noisy streets she cries out; at the entrance of the city gates she speaks:

22 "How long, O simple ones, will you love being simple? How long will scoffers delight in their scoffing and fools hate knowledge?

23 If you turn at my reproof, behold, I will pour out my spirit to you; I will make my words known to you.

24 Because I have called and you refused to listen, have stretched out my hand and no one has heeded,

25 because you have ignored all my counsel and would have none of my reproof*,

26 I also will laugh at your calamity; I will mock** when terror strikes you,

27 when terror strikes you like a storm and your calamity comes like a whirlwind***, when distress and anguish come upon you.

28 Then they will call upon me, but I will not answer; they will seek me diligently but will not find me.

29 Because they hated knowledge and did not choose the fear of the LORD,

30 would have none of my counsel and despised all my reproof,

---

* reproof [riprúːf] ⑨ 책망, 비난, 질책.
** mock [mɑk, mɔ(ː)k] ⑧ 조롱하다, 놀리다, 비난하다.
*** whirlwind [wɜːrlwind] ⑨ 회오리바람 ⑩ 정신없이 진행되는, 분주한.

31 therefore they shall eat the fruit of their way, and have their fill of their own devices.

32 For the simple are killed by their turning away, and the complacency of fools destroys them;

33 but whoever listens to me will dwell secure and will be at ease, without dread* of disaster."

★ dread [dred] ⑧ 두려워하다, 염려하다 ⑲ 공포, 불안.

암송 구절 해설

**The fear of the LORD is the beginning of knowledge;
fools despise wisdom and instruction(1:7).**

여호와를 경외하는 것이 지식의 근본이거늘
미련한 자는 지혜와 훈계를 멸시하느니라.

1장 7절은 잠언 전체를 포괄하는 주제라고 할 수 있습니다. 여호와를 경외하는 것은 그분의 공정한 심판을 두려워하며, 최고의 존경과 사랑으로 그분을 꼭 붙잡는 것입니다. 반대로 미련한 자들은 성경의 지혜를 경멸하는데, 이는 곧 주님을 거부하는 것입니다. 참된 지혜는 하나님을 경외하는 사람만이 얻을 수 있습니다.

하루 한 문장, 생각 쓰기

오늘 본문을 쓰면서 깨달은 지혜, 새롭게 다짐한 점,
떠오른 생각 등을 자유롭게 적어 보세요.

Proverbs 2

The Value of Wisdom

1 My son, if you receive my words and treasure up my commandments with you,

2 making your ear attentive to wisdom and inclining your heart to understanding;

3 yes, if you call out for insight and raise your voice for understanding,

4 if you seek it like silver and search for it as for hidden treasures,

5 then you will understand the fear of the LORD and find the knowledge of God.

6 For the LORD gives wisdom; from his mouth come knowledge and understanding;

7 he stores up sound wisdom for the upright; he is a shield to those who walk in integrity*,

8 guarding the paths of justice and watching over the way of his saints.

9 Then you will understand righteousness and justice and equity, every good path;

10 for wisdom will come into your heart, and knowledge will be pleasant to your soul;

11 discretion** will watch over you, understanding will guard you,

---

* integrity [intégrəti] ⑲ 진실성, 온전함.

** discretion [diskréʃən] ⑲ 결정권, 신중함, 근신.

12 delivering you from the way of evil, from men of perverted speech,

13 who forsake the paths of uprightness to walk in the ways of darkness,

14 who rejoice in doing evil and delight in the perverseness of evil,

15 men whose paths are crooked, and who are devious in their ways.

16 So you will be delivered from the forbidden woman, from the adulteress* with her smooth words,

17 who forsakes the companion of her youth and forgets the covenant of her God;

18 for her house sinks down to death, and her paths to the departed;

19 none who go to her come back, nor do they regain the paths of life.

20 So you will walk in the way of the good and keep to the paths of the righteous.

21 For the upright will inhabit the land, and those with integrity will remain in it,

22 but the wicked will be cut off from the land, and the treacherous will be rooted out of it.

---

* adulteress [ədʌltəris] ⑲ 음녀, 간음한 여자.

암송 구절 해설

He stores up sound wisdom for the upright;
he is a shield to those who walk in integrity(2:7).

그는 정직한 자를 위하여 완전한 지혜를 예비하시며
행실이 온전한 자에게 방패가 되시나니.

하나님과 바른 관계를 맺는 이들은 어리석은 결정을 내리지 않도록 보호를 받습니다. 성경은 그들을 정직한 자, 행실이 온전한 자, 그의 성도(8절)로 표현했는데, 이를 통해 성경의 지혜가 도덕적 차원과 언약적 차원을 둘 다 지니고 있음을 알 수 있습니다. 주님은 그들에게 완전한 지혜를 풍부하게 주시고, 곤경을 피할 수 있도록 지략도 주십니다.

오늘 본문을 쓰면서 깨달은 지혜, 새롭게 다짐한 점,
떠오른 생각 등을 자유롭게 적어 보세요.

Proverbs 3

Trust in the Lord with All Your Heart

1　My son, do not forget my teaching, but let your heart keep my commandments,

2　for length of days and years of life and peace they will add to you.

3　Let not steadfast* love and faithfulness forsake you; bind them around your neck; write them on the tablet of your heart.

4　So you will find favor and good success in the sight of God and man.

5　Trust in the LORD with all your heart, and do not lean on your own understanding.

6　In all your ways acknowledge him, and he will make straight your paths.

7　Be not wise in your own eyes; fear the LORD, and turn away from evil.

8　It will be healing to your flesh and refreshment to your bones.

9　Honor the LORD with your wealth and with the firstfruits of all your produce;

10　then your barns will be filled with** plenty, and your vats will be bursting with*** wine.

---

*　　steadfast [stedfæst] ⑧ 변함없는.

**　be filled with ∼로 가득 차다.

*** be bursting with ∼로 꽉 차다, ∼로 넘치다.

11 My son, do not despise* the LORD's discipline or be weary of his reproof**,

12 for the LORD reproves him whom he loves, as a father the son in whom he delights.

Blessed Is the One Who Finds Wisdom

13 Blessed is the one who finds wisdom, and the one who gets understanding,

14 for the gain from her is better than gain from silver and her profit better than gold.

15 She is more precious than jewels, and nothing you desire can compare with her.

16 Long life is in her right hand; in her left hand are riches and honor.

17 Her ways are ways of pleasantness, and all her paths are peace.

18 She is a tree of life to those who lay hold of her; those who hold her fast are called blessed.

19 The LORD by wisdom founded the earth; by understanding he established the heavens;

20 by his knowledge the deeps broke open, and the clouds drop down*** the dew.

---

* despise [dispáiz] ⑧ 경멸하다. 싫어하다.

** reproof [riprú:f] ⑨ 책망. 꾸지람.

*** drop down 쓰러지다. 떨어지다.

DAY 3

21 My son, do not lose sight of these—keep sound wisdom and discretion,

22 and they will be life for your soul and adornment* for your neck.

23 Then you will walk on your way securely, and your foot will not stumble**.

24 If you lie down, you will not be afraid; when you lie down, your sleep will be sweet.

25 Do not be afraid of sudden terror or of the ruin of the wicked, when it comes,

26 for the LORD will be your confidence and will keep your foot from being caught.

27 Do not withhold good from those to whom it is due, when it is in your power to do it.

28 Do not say to your neighbor, "Go, and come again, tomorrow I will give it"—when you have it with you.

29 Do not plan evil against your neighbor, who dwells trustingly*** beside you.

30 Do not contend with a man for no reason, when he has done you no harm.

* adornment [ədɔ́ːrnmənt] 명 장식. 꾸미기.
** stumble [stʌmbl] 통 넘어지다, 비틀거리다.
*** trustingly [trʌstiŋli] 부 신용하여, 안심하여.

31 Do not envy a man of violence and do not choose any of his ways,

32 for the devious* person is an abomination** to the LORD, but the upright are in his confidence.

33 The LORD's curse is on the house of the wicked, but he blesses the dwelling of the righteous.

34 Toward the scorners he is scornful, but to the humble he gives favor.

35 The wise will inherit honor, but fools get disgrace.

*   devious [díːviəs] ⓐ 정직하지 않은.
**   abomination [əbὰmənéiʃən] ⓝ 가증, 혐오스러운 것.

암송 구절 해설

**Trust in the LORD with all your heart,
and do not lean on your own understanding(3:5).**

너는 마음을 다하여 여호와를 신뢰하고
네 명철을 의지하지 말라.

하나님을 신뢰하는 것은 그분의 애정 어린 돌보심 속에서 평안히 쉬고, 그분의 능력을 온전히 의지하는 것입니다. 따라서 주님을 신뢰하는 자라면 자신의 명철을 의지하지 않을 것입니다. 오직 자신의 부족함을 인정하는 사람만이 하나님의 능력과 지혜를 이용할 수 있습니다.

오늘 본문을 쓰면서 깨달은 지혜, 새롭게 다짐한 점,
떠오른 생각 등을 자유롭게 적어 보세요.

Proverbs 4

A Father's Wise Instruction

1 Hear, O sons, a father's instruction, and be attentive, that you may gain insight,

2 for I give you good precepts*; do not forsake my teaching.

3 When I was a son with my father, tender, the only one in the sight of my mother,

4 he taught me and said to me, "Let your heart hold fast my words; keep my commandments, and live.

5 Get wisdom; get insight; do not forget, and do not turn away from** the words of my mouth.

6 Do not forsake her, and she will keep you; love her, and she will guard you.

7 The beginning of wisdom is this: Get wisdom, and whatever you get, get insight.

8 Prize her highly, and she will exalt you; she will honor you if you embrace her.

9 She will place on your head a graceful garland; she will bestow*** on you a beautiful crown."

10 Hear, my son, and accept my words, that the years of your life may be many.

---

* precept [priˈsept] 몡 교훈, 가르침.
** turn away from ~을 외면하다.
*** bestow [bistóu] 통 주다, 들이다.

11 I have taught you the way of wisdom; I have led you in the paths of uprightness*.

12 When you walk, your step will not be hampered**, and if you run, you will not stumble.

13 Keep hold of instruction; do not let go; guard her, for she is your life.

14 Do not enter the path of the wicked, and do not walk in the way of the evil.

15 Avoid it; do not go on it; turn away from it and pass on.

16 For they cannot sleep unless they have done wrong; they are robbed*** of sleep unless they have made someone stumble.

17 For they eat the bread of wickedness and drink the wine of violence.

18 But the path of the righteous is like the light of dawn, which shines brighter and brighter until full day.

19 The way of the wicked is like deep darkness; they do not know over what they stumble.

20 My son, be attentive to my words; incline your ear to my sayings.

---

* uprightness [ʌpraɪtnəs] ⑲ 강직함. 정직함.

** hamper [hǽmpər] ⑲ 방해. 문제. 좌절 ⑤ 방해하다. 저지하다.

*** be robbed 강도를 만나다. 빼앗기다.

21 Let them not escape from your sight; keep them within your heart.

22 For they are life to those who find them, and healing to all their flesh.

23 <u>Keep your heart with all vigilance*, for from it flow the springs of life.</u>

24 Put away from you crooked speech, and put devious talk far from you.

25 Let your eyes look directly forward, and your gaze be straight before you.

26 Ponder** the path of your feet; then all your ways will be sure.

27 Do not swerve to the right or to the left; turn your foot away from evil.

* vigilance [vídʒələns] ⑱ 경계, 불면증.
** ponder [pɑ́ndər] ⑧ 숙고하다, 깊이 생각하다.

암송 구절 해설

**Keep your heart with all vigilance,
for from it flow the springs of life**(4:23).

모든 지킬 만한 것 중에 더욱 네 마음을 지키라
생명의 근원이 이에서 남이니라.

이 표현은 우리의 모든 행동이 마음에서 비롯되고 생겨난다는 것을 암시합니다. 그러므로 우리는 마음을 지키는 것을 우선순위로 삼지 않으면 안 됩니다. 무엇보다 악을 꾀하지 않도록 마음을 부지런히 지켜야 합니다.

오늘 본문을 쓰면서 깨달은 지혜, 새롭게 다짐한 점,
떠오른 생각 등을 자유롭게 적어 보세요.

DATE. . . .

Proverbs 5

Warning Against Adultery

1 My son, be attentive to my wisdom; incline* your ear to my understanding,

2 that you may keep discretion, and your lips may guard knowledge.

3 For the lips of a forbidden woman drip honey, and her speech is smoother than oil,

4 but in the end she is bitter as wormwood, sharp as a two-edged sword.

5 Her feet go down to death; her steps follow the path to Sheol;

6 she does not ponder the path of life; her ways wander, and she does not know it.

7 And now, O sons, listen to me, and do not depart from the words of my mouth.

8 Keep your way far from her, and do not go near the door of her house,

9 lest you give your honor to others and your years to the merciless,

10 lest strangers take their fill of your strength, and your labors go to the house of a foreigner,

11 and at the end of your life you groan**, when your flesh and body are consumed,

12 and you say, "How I hated discipline***, and my heart despised reproof!

---

* incline [inkláin] 명 생각 동 ~ 쪽으로 기울다.
** groan [groun] 동 괴로워하다, 한탄하다.
*** discipline [dísəplin] 명 훈련, 훈계, 규율.

13 I did not listen to the voice of my teachers or incline my ear to my instructors.

14 I am at the brink of utter ruin in the assembled congregation."

15 Drink water from your own cistern, flowing water from your own well.

16 Should your springs be scattered abroad, streams of water in the streets?

17 Let them be for yourself alone, and not for strangers with you.

18 Let your fountain be blessed, and rejoice in the wife of your youth,

19 a lovely deer, a graceful doe. Let her breasts fill you at all times with delight; be intoxicated always in her love.

20 Why should you be intoxicated, my son, with a forbidden woman and embrace the bosom of an adulteress?

21 For a man's ways are before the eyes of the LORD, and he ponders all his paths.

22 The iniquities of the wicked ensnare him, and he is held fast in the cords of his sin.

23 He dies for lack of discipline, and because of his great folly he is led astray.

암송 구절 해설

For a man's ways are before the eyes of the LORD,
and he ponders all his paths(5:21).

대저 사람의 길은 여호와의 눈앞에 있나니
그가 그 사람의 모든 길을 평탄하게 하시느니라.

5장은 성적인 죄에 대해 이야기합니다. 21-23절에서 아버지는 아들이 음녀를 피해야 하는 이유를 더욱 강조합니다. 여호와의 눈앞에 있다는 말은 하나님이 전지하시기 때문에 어디에서 어떤 죄를 지어도 그분의 심판을 피할 수 없다는 뜻입니다. 우리는 죄에 대한 심판을 피할 수 없다는 사실을 기억하고 지혜롭고 평탄한 길을 선택해야 합니다. 그것이 여호와를 경외하는 길입니다.

✏️ 하루 한 문장, 생각 쓰기

오늘 본문을 쓰면서 깨달은 지혜, 새롭게 다짐한 점.
떠오른 생각 등을 자유롭게 적어 보세요.

Proverbs 6

Practical Warnings

1 My son, if you have put up security for your neighbor, have given your pledge* for a stranger,

2 if you are snared in the words of your mouth, caught in the words of your mouth,

3 then do this, my son, and save yourself, for you have come into the hand of your neighbor: go, hasten, and plead urgently with your neighbor.

4 Give your eyes no sleep and your eyelids no slumber**;

5 save yourself like a gazelle from the hand of the hunter, like a bird from the hand of the fowler.

6 Go to the ant, O sluggard***; consider her ways, and be wise.

7 Without having any chief, officer, or ruler,

8 she prepares her bread in summer and gathers her food in harvest.

9 How long will you lie there, O sluggard? When will you arise from your sleep?

10 A little sleep, a little slumber, a little folding of the hands to rest,

---

* pledge [pledʒ] ⑧ 약속하다. 담보하다.

** slumber [slʌmbər] ⑨ 선잠 ⑧ 잠시 졸다.

*** sluggard [slʌgərd] ⑨ 게으름뱅이.

11 and poverty* will come upon you like a robber, and want like an armed man.

12 A worthless person, a wicked man, goes about with crooked** speech,

13 winks with his eyes, signals with his feet, points with his finger,

14 with perverted heart devises evil, continually sowing discord;

15 therefore calamity will come upon him suddenly; in a moment he will be broken beyond healing.

16 There are six things that the LORD hates, seven that are an abomination to him:

17 haughty eyes, a lying tongue, and hands that shed innocent blood,

18 a heart that devises wicked plans, feet that make haste to run to evil,

19 a false witness who breathes out lies, and one who sows discord*** among brothers.

---

*   poverty [pάvərti] 몡 빈곤. 가난.

**   crooked [krúkid] 혱 구부러진. 비뚤어진.

*** discord [dískɔːrd] 몡 불화. 불일치. 내분.

Warnings Against Adultery

20 My son, keep your father's commandment, and forsake not your mother's teaching.

21 Bind them on your heart always; tie them around your neck.

22 When you walk, they will lead you; when you lie down, they will watch over you; and when you awake, they will talk with you.

23 For the commandment is a lamp and the teaching a light, and the reproofs of discipline are the way of life,

24 to preserve you from the evil woman, from the smooth tongue of the adulteress.

25 Do not desire her beauty in your heart, and do not let her capture you with her eyelashes*;

26 for the price of a prostitute** is only a loaf of bread, but a married woman hunts down a precious life.

27 Can a man carry fire next to his chest and his clothes not be burned?

28 Or can one walk on hot coals and his feet not be scorched***?

29 So is he who goes in to his neighbor's wife; none who touches her will go unpunished.

30 People do not despise a thief if he steals to satisfy his appetite when he is hungry,

---

*   eyelash [ailæʃ] ⑱ 속눈썹.
**   prostitute [prάstətjùːt] ⑱ 매춘부 ⑧ 매춘하다.
*** scorched [skɔːrtʃt] ⑲ 탄, 그을은.

31 but if he is caught, he will pay sevenfold*; he will give all the goods of his house.

32 He who commits adultery** lacks sense; he who does it destroys himself.

33 He will get wounds and dishonor, and his disgrace will not be wiped away.

34 For jealousy makes a man furious, and he will not spare when he takes revenge.

35 He will accept no compensation***; he will refuse though you multiply gifts.

---

* sevenfold [sévnfòuld] ⑧ 7배의.

** adultery [ədʌltəri] ⑱ 간음. 부정.

*** compensation [kàmpənséiʃən] ⑱ 보상. 대가.

암송 구절 해설

For the commandment is a lamp and the teaching a light,
and the reproofs of discipline are the way of life(6:23).

대저 명령은 등불이요 법은 빛이요
훈계의 책망은 곧 생명의 길이라.

주님의 계명은 등불이며 빛이기 때문에 주님의 훈계와 말씀을 항상 마음에 둬야 합니다(참고. 시 19:8; 119:105). 이러한 지혜는 우리 삶의 훌륭한 동반자입니다. 그것이 생명의 길을 비추고, 우리를 징계하여 위험에 빠지지 않게 보호하기 때문입니다.

오늘 본문을 쓰면서 깨달은 지혜, 새롭게 다짐한 점,
떠오른 생각 등을 자유롭게 적어 보세요.

Proverbs 7

Warning Against the Adulteress

1 My son, keep my words and treasure up my commandments with you;

2 keep my commandments and live; keep my teaching as the apple of your eye;

3 bind them on your fingers; write them on the tablet of your heart.

4 Say to wisdom, "You are my sister," and call insight your intimate friend,

5 to keep you from the forbidden woman, from the adulteress with her smooth words.

6 For at the window of my house I have looked out through my lattice*,

7 and I have seen among the simple, I have perceived among the youths, a young man lacking sense,

8 passing along the street near her corner, taking the road to her house

9 in the twilight**, in the evening, at the time of night and darkness.

10 And behold, the woman meets him, dressed as a prostitute, wily of heart.

---

* lattice [lǽtis] ⑲ 격자창(창살을 바둑판처럼 가로세로가 일정한 간격으로 직각이 되게 짠 창).

** twilight [twáilàit] ⑲ 황혼. 석양.

11 She is loud and wayward*; her feet do not stay at home;

12 now in the street, now in the market, and at every corner she lies in wait.

13 She seizes him and kisses him, and with bold face she says to him,

14 "I had to offer sacrifices**, and today I have paid my vows;

15 so now I have come out to meet you, to seek you eagerly, and I have found you.

16 I have spread my couch with coverings, colored linens from Egyptian linen;

17 I have perfumed my bed with myrrh***, aloes, and cinnamon.

18 Come, let us take our fill of love till morning; let us delight ourselves with love.

19 For my husband is not at home; he has gone on a long journey;

20 he took a bag of money with him; at full moon he will come home."

---

*   wayward [wéiwərd] ⑧ 변덕스러운, 고집불통인.

**   sacrifice [sǽkrəfàis] ⑨ 희생, 제물, 화목제.

*** myrrh [məːr] ⑨ 몰약.

21 With much seductive speech she persuades him; with her smooth talk she compels him.

22 All at once he follows her, as an ox goes to the slaughter*, or as a stag** is caught fast

23 till an arrow pierces its liver***; as a bird rushes into a snare; he does not know that it will cost him his life.

24 And now, O sons, listen to me, and be attentive to the words of my mouth.

25 Let not your heart turn aside to her ways; do not stray into her paths,

26 for many a victim has she laid low, and all her slain are a mighty throng.

27 Her house is the way to Sheol, going down to the chambers of death.

---

*   slaughter [slɔ́:tər] ⑲ 도살, 도축 ⑧ 도살하다, 도축하다.

**   stag [stæg] ⑲ 남자, 수컷.

*** liver [lívər] ⑲ 간.

암송 구절 해설

Keep my commandments and live;
keep my teaching as the apple of your eye(7:2).
내 계명을 지켜 살며 내 법을 네 눈동자처럼 지키라.

아버지는 다시 한번 아들에게 자신의 계명을 지키고 간직하라고 권고합니다(1절). 아들은 자신의 예민한 눈동자를 보호하듯 하나님 아버지의 계명을 최대의 관심사로 삼아 자신을 지키지 않으면 안 됩니다.

오늘 본문을 쓰면서 깨달은 지혜, 새롭게 다짐한 점.
떠오른 생각 등을 자유롭게 적어 보세요.

Proverbs 8

The Blessings of Wisdom

1 Does not wisdom call? Does not understanding raise her voice?

2 On the heights beside the way, at the crossroads she takes her stand;

3 beside the gates in front of the town, at the entrance of the portals* she cries aloud:

4 "To you, O men, I call, and my cry is to the children of man.

5 O simple ones, learn prudence; O fools, learn sense.

6 Hear, for I will speak noble things, and from my lips will come what is right,

7 for my mouth will utter** truth; wickedness is an abomination to my lips.

8 All the words of my mouth are righteous; there is nothing twisted*** or crooked in them.

9 They are all straight to him who understands, and right to those who find knowledge.

10 Take my instruction instead of silver, and knowledge rather than choice gold,

---

*   portals [pɔ́:rtlz] ⑱ 정문. 시초.

** utter [ʌ́tər] ⑧ 말하다. 입 밖에 내다. 유통하다.

*** twisted [twístid] ⑱ 비뚤어진. 뒤틀린. 굽은.

11 for wisdom is better than jewels, and all that you may desire cannot compare with her.

12 "I, wisdom, dwell with prudence, and I find knowledge and discretion.

13 The fear of the LORD is hatred of evil. Pride and arrogance and the way of evil and perverted* speech I hate.

14 I have counsel and sound wisdom; I have insight; I have strength.

15 By me kings reign, and rulers decree** what is just;

16 by me princes rule, and nobles, all who govern justly.

17 I love those who love me, and those who seek me diligently find me.

18 Riches and honor are with me, enduring wealth and righteousness.

19 My fruit is better than gold, even fine gold, and my yield than choice silver.

20 I walk in the way of righteousness, in the paths of justice,

21 granting an inheritance*** to those who love me, and filling their treasuries.

---

* perverted [pərvə́ːrtid] ⑲ 그릇된. 잘못된.
** decree [dikríː] ⑲ 법령. 명령 ⑤ 정하다. 명하다.
*** inheritance [inhérətəns] ⑲ 상속. 계승.

22 "The LORD possessed me at the beginning of his work, the first of his acts of old.

23 Ages ago I was set up, at the first, before the beginning of the earth.

24 When there were no depths I was brought forth, when there were no springs abounding with water.

25 Before the mountains had been shaped, before the hills, I was brought forth,

26 before he had made the earth with its fields, or the first of the dust of the world.

27 When he established the heavens, I was there; when he drew a circle on the face of the deep,

28 when he made firm the skies above, when he established the fountains of the deep,

29 when he assigned to the sea its limit, so that the waters might not transgress* his command, when he marked out** the foundations of the earth,

---

*   transgress [trænsgrés] ⑧ 어기다. 거스르다.

**   mark out ~을 표시하다. ~을 그리다.

30   then I was beside him, like a master workman, and I was daily his delight, rejoicing before him always,

31   rejoicing in his inhabited world and delighting in the children of man.

32   "And now, O sons, listen to me: blessed are those who keep my ways.

33   Hear instruction and be wise, and do not neglect* it.

34   Blessed is the one who listens to me, watching daily at my gates, waiting beside my doors.

35   For whoever finds me finds life and obtains favor from the LORD,

36   but he who fails to find me injures** himself; all who hate me love death."

*   neglect [niglékt] ⑧ 무시하다. 소홀히 하다.

**   injure [índʒər] ⑧ 상처를 입히다. 다치게 하다.

암송 구절 해설

The fear of the LORD is hatred of evil. Pride and arrogance and the way of evil and perverted speech I hate(8:13).

여호와를 경외하는 것은 악을 미워하는 것이라
나는 교만과 거만과 악한 행실과 패역한 입을 미워하느니라.

지혜가 있는 곳에는 명철과 지식과 근신이 함께 있습니다. 지혜의 이러한 속성들은 여호와를 경외하는 것과 결코 분리되지 않습니다. 여호와를 경외함은 다양한 형태의 악, 즉 교만과 거만과 악한 행실과 패역한 말을 항상 미워하는 것과 같습니다. 우리는 참된 지혜와 단순한 영리함을 혼동해서는 안 됩니다. '똑똑하고 영리한 사람이 특히 보이기 쉬운' 건방진 교만은 참된 지혜가 아닙니다.

오늘 본문을 쓰면서 깨달은 지혜, 새롭게 다짐한 점,
떠오른 생각 등을 자유롭게 적어 보세요.

Proverbs 9

The Way of Wisdom

1 Wisdom has built her house; she has hewn her seven pillars.

2 She has slaughtered her beasts; she has mixed her wine; she has also set her table.

3 She has sent out her young women to call from the highest places in the town,

4 "Whoever is simple, let him turn in here!" To him who lacks sense she says,

5 "Come, eat of my bread and drink of the wine I have mixed.

6 Leave your simple ways, and live, and walk in the way of insight."

7 Whoever corrects a scoffer* gets himself abuse, and he who reproves a wicked man incurs injury.

8 Do not reprove a scoffer, or he will hate you; reprove a wise man, and he will love you.

9 Give instruction to a wise man, and he will be still wiser; teach a righteous man, and he will increase in learning.

10 The fear of the LORD is the beginning of wisdom, and the knowledge of the Holy One is insight.

---

*   scoffer [skɑ́fər] ⑲ 비웃는 사람, 조소하는 사람.

11 For by me your days will be multiplied, and years will be added to your life.

12 If you are wise, you are wise for yourself; if you scoff, you alone will bear it.

The Way of Folly

13 The woman Folly is loud; she is seductive and knows nothing.

14 She sits at the door of her house; she takes a seat on the highest places of the town,

15 calling to those who pass by, who are going straight on their way,

16 "Whoever is simple, let him turn in here!" And to him who lacks sense she says,

17 "Stolen water is sweet, and bread eaten in secret is pleasant."

18 But he does not know that the dead are there, that her guests are in the depths of Sheol.

암송 구절 해설

**If you are wise, you are wise for yourself;
if you scoff, you alone will bear it(9:12).**

네가 만일 지혜로우면 그 지혜가 네게 유익할 것이나
네가 만일 거만하면 너 홀로 해를 당하리라.

지혜는 생명을 가져다줍니다(11절). 지혜를 선택했을 때 가장 큰 이득을 보는 사람은 그것을 선택한 자신입니다. 이 말은 어리석음이 사망을 초래함을 암시하기도 합니다. 따라서 지혜를 무시하는 거만한 사람은 남을 탓할 게 아니라 자신을 탓해야 합니다. 자기 홀로 어리석음의 열매를 맺을 것이기 때문입니다.

오늘 본문을 쓰면서 깨달은 지혜, 새롭게 다짐한 점,
떠오른 생각 등을 자유롭게 적어 보세요.

Proverbs 10

The Proverbs of Solomon

1   The proverbs of Solomon. A wise son makes a glad father, but a foolish son is a sorrow to his mother.

2   Treasures gained by wickedness do not profit, but righteousness delivers from death.

3   The LORD does not let the righteous go hungry, but he thwarts* the craving of the wicked.

4   A slack** hand causes poverty, but the hand of the diligent makes rich.

5   He who gathers in summer is a prudent*** son, but he who sleeps in harvest is a son who brings shame.

6   Blessings are on the head of the righteous, but the mouth of the wicked conceals violence.

7   The memory of the righteous is a blessing, but the name of the wicked will rot.

8   The wise of heart will receive commandments, but a babbling fool will come to ruin.

9   Whoever walks in integrity walks securely, but he who makes his ways crooked will be found out.

10 Whoever winks the eye causes trouble, and a babbling fool will come to ruin.

---

*   thwart [θwɔːrt] ⑧ 좌절시키다. 방해하다.
**   slack [slæk] ⑲ 느슨한. 꾸물거리는 ⑲ 게으름. 부진.
*** prudent [prúːdnt] ⑲ 신중한. 분별 있는.

11 The mouth of the righteous is a fountain of life, but the mouth of the wicked conceals violence.

12 Hatred stirs up strife*, but love covers all offenses.

13 On the lips of him who has understanding, wisdom is found, but a rod is for the back of him who lacks sense.

14 The wise lay up knowledge, but the mouth of a fool brings ruin near.

15 A rich man's wealth is his strong city; the poverty of the poor is their ruin.

16 The wage of the righteous leads to life, the gain of the wicked to sin.

17 Whoever heeds instruction is on the path to life, but he who rejects reproof leads others astray**.

18 The one who conceals hatred has lying lips, and whoever utters slander is a fool.

19 When words are many, transgression is not lacking, but whoever restrains his lips is prudent.

20 The tongue of the righteous is choice silver; the heart of the wicked is of little worth.

---

*   strife [straif] 몡 다툼, 분쟁, 갈등.
**   astray [əstréi] 믯몡 옳은 길에서 벗어난, 길을 잃은.

21 The lips of the righteous feed many, but fools die for lack of sense.

22 The blessing of the LORD makes rich, and he adds no sorrow with it.

23 Doing wrong is like a joke to a fool, but wisdom is pleasure to a man of understanding.

24 What the wicked dreads will come upon him, but the desire of the righteous will be granted.

25 When the tempest* passes, the wicked is no more, but the righteous is established forever.

26 Like vinegar** to the teeth and smoke to the eyes, so is the sluggard to those who send him.

27 The fear of the LORD prolongs life, but the years of the wicked will be short.

28 The hope of the righteous brings joy, but the expectation of the wicked will perish***.

---

*   tempest [témpist] 명 폭풍우 동 격렬하게 휩쓸다.

**   vinegar [vínəgər] 명 식초.

*** perish [périʃ] 동 사라지다, 죽다.

29 The way of the LORD is a stronghold* to the blameless**, but destruction to evildoers***.

30 The righteous will never be removed, but the wicked will not dwell in the land.

31 The mouth of the righteous brings forth wisdom, but the perverse tongue will be cut off.

32 The lips of the righteous know what is acceptable, but the mouth of the wicked, what is perverse.

---

*   stronghold [strɔ:ŋhould] 몡 요새, 본거지.

**   blameless [bléimlis] 몡 나무랄 데 없는, 떳떳한.

*** evildoer [ivəlduər] 몡 악인, 나쁜 짓을 하는 사람.

암송 구절 해설

The proverbs of Solomon. A wise son makes a glad father,
but a foolish son is a sorrow to his mother(10:1).

솔로몬의 잠언이라 지혜로운 아들은 아비를 기쁘게 하거니와
미련한 아들은 어미의 근심이니라.

10장 1절은 부모와 자녀의 관계를 예로 들어 지혜와 어리석음의 차이를 보여 줍니다. 1절에서는 아들이 아비와 어미를 사랑하는 마음으로 지혜를 택하도록 동기를 부여합니다. 자녀를 향한 부모의 사랑을 조금이라도 헤아리는 자녀라면 지혜를 택할 것입니다. 그가 어느 쪽을 택하는가는 부모에게 기쁨을 주기도 하고 근심을 주기도 할 것입니다. 선택은 홀로 하는 것이지만, 그 선택이 자기 혼자만의 일이 될 수는 없다는 것을 기억해야 합니다.

오늘 본문을 쓰면서 깨달은 지혜, 새롭게 다짐한 점,
떠오른 생각 등을 자유롭게 적어 보세요.

Proverbs 11

1　A false balance is an abomination to the LORD, but a just weight is his delight.

2　When pride comes, then comes disgrace, but with the humble is wisdom.

3　The integrity of the upright guides them, but the crookedness of the treacherous* destroys them.

4　Riches do not profit in the day of wrath**, but righteousness delivers from death.

5　The righteousness of the blameless keeps his way straight, but the wicked falls by his own wickedness.

6　The righteousness of the upright delivers them, but the treacherous are taken captive by their lust.

7　When the wicked dies, his hope will perish, and the expectation of wealth perishes too.

8　The righteous is delivered from trouble, and the wicked walks into it instead.

9　With his mouth the godless man would destroy his neighbor, but by knowledge the righteous are delivered.

10　When it goes well with the righteous, the city rejoices, and when the wicked perish there are shouts of gladness.

11　By the blessing of the upright a city is exalted, but by the mouth of the wicked it is overthrown.

---

*　treacherous [trétʃərəs] ⑱ 반역하는, 믿을 수 없는.

**　wrath [ræθ] ⑱ 진노, 분노, 복수.

12 Whoever belittles his neighbor lacks sense, but a man of understanding remains silent.

13 Whoever goes about slandering* reveals secrets, but he who is trustworthy** in spirit keeps a thing covered.

14 Where there is no guidance, a people falls, but in an abundance of counselors there is safety.

15 Whoever puts up security for a stranger will surely suffer harm, but he who hates striking hands in pledge is secure.

16 A gracious woman gets honor, and violent men get riches.

17 A man who is kind benefits himself, but a cruel man hurts himself.

18 The wicked earns deceptive wages, but one who sows righteousness gets a sure reward.

19 Whoever is steadfast in righteousness will live, but he who pursues evil will die.

20 Those of crooked heart are an abomination to the LORD, but those of blameless ways are his delight.

21 Be assured, an evil person will not go unpunished, but the offspring of the righteous will be delivered.

22 Like a gold ring in a pig's snout*** is a beautiful woman without discretion.

---

* slander [slǽndər] ⑲ 비방, 욕 ⑤ 비방하다, 헐뜯다.
** trustworthy [trʌstwɜːrði] ⑲ 신실한, 믿을 수 있는.
*** snout [snaut] ⑲ 코, 주둥이.

23 The desire of the righteous ends only in good, the expectation of the wicked in wrath.

24 One gives freely, yet grows all the richer; another withholds what he should give, and only suffers want.

25 Whoever brings blessing will be enriched, and one who waters will himself be watered.

26 The people curse him who holds back grain, but a blessing is on the head of him who sells it.

27 Whoever diligently seeks good seeks favor, but evil comes to him who searches for it.

28 Whoever trusts in his riches will fall, but the righteous will flourish* like a green leaf.

29 Whoever troubles his own household will inherit the wind, and the fool will be servant to the wise of heart.

30 The fruit of the righteous is a tree of life, and whoever captures souls is wise.

31 If the righteous is repaid on earth, how much more the wicked and the sinner!

---

* flourish [fláːriʃ] ⑧ 번성하다, 무성하다.

암송 구절 해설

**Whoever brings blessing will be enriched,
and one who waters will himself be watered**(11:25).

구제를 좋아하는 자는 풍족하여질 것이요
남을 윤택하게 하는 자는 자기도 윤택하여지리라.

지혜로운 사람은 특히 궁핍한 사람들에게 아낌없이 베풉니다. 그는 다른 이에게 인색한 구두쇠와 대조를 이룹니다. 역설적이게도 후히 베푸는 사람의 재산은 더 많아지는 반면, 구두쇠의 재산은 점점 줄어서 가난하게 될 뿐입니다(24절).

하루 한 문장, 생각 쓰기

오늘 본문을 쓰면서 깨달은 지혜, 새롭게 다짐한 점,
떠오른 생각 등을 자유롭게 적어 보세요.

Proverbs 12

1   Whoever loves discipline loves knowledge, but he who hates reproof is stupid.

2   A good man obtains favor from the LORD, but a man of evil devices he condemns.

3   No one is established by wickedness, but the root of the righteous will never be moved.

4   An excellent wife is the crown of her husband, but she who brings shame is like rottenness in his bones.

5   The thoughts of the righteous are just; the counsels of the wicked are deceitful*.

6   The words of the wicked lie in wait for blood, but the mouth of the up right delivers them.

7   The wicked are overthrown and are no more, but the house of the righteous will stand.

8   A man is commended according to his good sense, but one of twisted mind is despised.

9   Better to be lowly and have a servant than to play the great man and lack bread.

10 Whoever is righteous has regard for the life of his beast, but the mercy of the wicked is cruel.

---

*   deceitful [disíːtfəl] ⑧ 속이는, 기만하는.

11 Whoever works his land will have plenty of* bread, but he who follows worthless pursuits lacks sense.

12 Whoever is wicked covets the spoil of evildoers, but the root of the righteous bears fruit.

13 An evil man is ensnared** by the transgression of his lips, but the righteous escapes from trouble.

14 From the fruit of his mouth a man is satisfied with good, and the work of a man's hand comes back to him.

15 The way of a fool is right in his own eyes, but a wise man listens to advice.

16 The vexation*** of a fool is known at once, but the prudent ignores an insult.

17 Whoever speaks the truth gives honest evidence, but a false witness utters deceit.

18 There is one whose rash words are like sword thrusts, but the tongue of the wise brings healing.

19 Truthful lips endure forever, but a lying tongue is but for a moment.

20 Deceit is in the heart of those who devise evil, but those who plan peace have joy.

---

*   plenty of 많은, 충분한.
**   ensnare [insnéər] ⑧ 유혹하다, 덫으로 잡다.
*** vexation [vekséiʃən] ⑲ 짜증, 괴로움.

21 No ill befalls the righteous, but the wicked are filled with trouble.

22 Lying lips are an abomination to the LORD, but those who act faithfully are his delight.

23 A prudent man conceals knowledge, but the heart of fools proclaims folly.

24 The hand of the diligent will rule, while the slothful will be put to forced labor.

25 Anxiety in a man's heart weighs him down, but a good word makes him glad.

26 One who is righteous is a guide to his neighbor, but the way of the wicked leads them astray.

27 Whoever is slothful* will not roast his game, but the diligent man will get precious wealth.

28 In the path of righteousness is life, and in its pathway** there is no death.

＊ slothful [slɔ́:θfəl] ⑧ 게으른, 느린.

＊＊ pathway [pǽθwèi] ⑧ 오솔길, 좁은 길, 통로.

암송 구절 해설

**Anxiety in a man's heart weighs him down,
but a good word makes him glad**(12:25).

근심이 사람의 마음에 있으면 그것으로 번뇌하게 되나
선한 말은 그것을 즐겁게 하느니라.

선한 말, 즉 격려하는 말에는 힘이 있어서 마음을 번뇌하게 하는 근심의 해독제가 됩니다. 또한 앞날을 더 멀리 내다보게 해 줄 뿐만 아니라, 근심의 원인을 직시할 수 있도록 힘을 북돋우는 등 상황에 따라 다양한 형식으로 좋은 영향을 끼칩니다.

오늘 본문을 쓰면서 깨달은 지혜, 새롭게 다짐한 점,
떠오른 생각 등을 자유롭게 적어 보세요.

Proverbs 13

1 A wise son hears his father's instruction, but a scoffer does not listen to rebuke.

2 From the fruit of his mouth a man eats what is good, but the desire of the treacherous is for violence*.

3 Whoever guards his mouth preserves his life; he who opens wide his lips comes to ruin.

4 The soul of the sluggard craves** and gets nothing, while the soul of the diligent is richly supplied.

5 The righteous hates falsehood, but the wicked brings shame and disgrace.

6 Righteousness guards him whose way is blameless, but sin overthrows the wicked.

7 One pretends to be rich, yet has nothing; another pretends to be poor, yet has great wealth.

8 The ransom of a man's life is his wealth, but a poor man hears no threat.

9 The light of the righteous rejoices, but the lamp of the wicked will be put out.

10 By insolence*** comes nothing but strife, but with those who take advice is wisdom.

---

*   violence [váiələns] ⑱ 폭력, 범죄, 분쟁, 테러.

**   crave [kreiv] ⑧ 갈망하다, 열망하다, 간청하다.

*** insolence [ínsələns] ⑲ 오만, 무례.

11 Wealth gained hastily* will dwindle**, but whoever gathers little by little will increase it.

12 Hope deferred makes the heart sick, but a desire fulfilled is a tree of life.

13 Whoever despises the word brings destruction on himself, but he who reveres the commandment will be rewarded.

14 The teaching of the wise is a fountain of life, that one may turn away from the snares of death.

15 Good sense wins favor, but the way of the treacherous is their ruin.

16 Every prudent man acts with knowledge, but a fool flaunts*** his folly.

17 A wicked messenger falls into trouble, but a faithful envoy brings healing.

18 Poverty and disgrace come to him who ignores instruction, but whoever heeds reproof is honored.

19 A desire fulfilled is sweet to the soul, but to turn away from evil is an abomination to fools.

20 Whoever walks with the wise becomes wise, but the companion of fools will suffer harm.

---

*   hastily [héistili] ⑨ 급히, 서둘러서.
**   dwindle [dwíndl] ⑧ 줄어들다, 점점 작아지다.
*** flaunt [flɔːnt] ⑧ 과시하다, 거드름을 피우다.

21 Disaster* pursues sinners, but the righteous are rewarded with good.

22 A good man leaves an inheritance to his children's children, but the sinner's wealth is laid up for the righteous.

23 The fallow ground of the poor would yield much food, but it is swept away** through injustice.

24 Whoever spares the rod hates his son, but he who loves him is diligent to discipline him.

25 The righteous has enough to satisfy his appetite***, but the belly of the wicked suffers want.

---

* disaster [dizǽstər] ⑲ 재앙, 재난, 사고.

** sweep away 휩쓸어 가다.

*** appetite [ǽpətàit] ⑲ 식욕, 성향.

암송 구절 해설

**Wealth gained hastily will dwindle,
but whoever gathers little by little will increase it**(13:11).

망령되이 얻은 재물은 줄어가고
손으로 모은 것은 늘어가느니라.

부를 축적하는 일에서 인내의 장점이 드러납니다. 때때로 게으른 사람이 부를 창출하기도 하지만 그것은 오래가지 못합니다. 불건전한 수단으로 축적하거나 너무 쉽게 얻은 재산은 줄어들게 마련입니다. 반면에 열심히 끈기 있게 일하는 지혜로운 사람의 재산은 점점 늘어납니다.

오늘 본문을 쓰면서 깨달은 지혜, 새롭게 다짐한 점.
떠오른 생각 등을 자유롭게 적어 보세요.

Proverbs 14

1 The wisest of women builds her house, but folly with her own hands tears it down.

2 Whoever walks in uprightness fears the LORD, but he who is devious in his ways despises him.

3 By the mouth of a fool comes a rod for his back, but the lips of the wise will preserve them.

4 Where there are no oxen, the manger is clean, but abundant* crops come by the strength of the ox.

5 A faithful witness does not lie, but a false witness breathes out lies.

6 A scoffer seeks wisdom in vain, but knowledge is easy for a man of understanding.

7 Leave the presence of a fool, for there you do not meet words of knowledge.

8 The wisdom of the prudent is to discern his way, but the folly of fools is deceiving.

9 Fools mock at the guilt offering, but the upright enjoy acceptance.

10 The heart knows its own bitterness**, and no stranger shares its joy.

---

*　abundant [əbʌ́ndənt] ⑱ 풍부한, 남아도는.

**　bitterness [bítərnis] ⑱ 괴로움, 쓴맛.

11 The house of the wicked will be destroyed, but the tent of the upright will flourish.

12 There is a way that seems right to a man, but its end is the way to death.

13 Even in laughter the heart may ache, and the end of joy may be grief.

14 The backslider* in heart will be filled with the fruit of his ways, and a good man will be filled with the fruit of his ways.

15 The simple believes everything, but the prudent gives thought to his steps.

16 One who is wise is cautious and turns away from evil, but a fool is reckless and careless.

17 A man of quick temper acts foolishly, and a man of evil devices is hated.

18 The simple inherit folly, but the prudent are crowned with knowledge.

19 The evil bow down before the good, the wicked at the gates of the righteous.

20 The poor is disliked even by his neighbor, but the rich has many friends.

---

*   backslider [bǽkslàidər] 몡 배교자, 이전의 행실로 되돌아간 사람.

21 Whoever despises his neighbor is a sinner, but blessed is he who is generous to the poor.

22 Do they not go astray who devise evil? Those who devise good meet steadfast love and faithfulness.

23 In all toil* there is profit, but mere talk tends only to poverty.

24 The crown of the wise is their wealth, but the folly of fools brings folly.

25 A truthful witness saves lives, but one who breathes out lies is deceitful.

26 In the fear of the LORD one has strong confidence, and his children will have a refuge.

27 The fear of the LORD is a fountain of life, that one may turn away from the snares of death.

28 In a multitude of people is the glory of a king, but without people a prince is ruined.

29 Whoever is slow to anger has great understanding, but he who has a hasty temper exalts folly.

30 A tranquil** heart gives life to the flesh, but envy makes the bones rot.

---

* toil [tɔil] 몡 수고, 노력 툉 힘서 일하다, 애쓰다.
** tranquil [trǽŋkwil] 혱 조용한, 고요한, 평온한.

31 Whoever oppresses a poor man insults his Maker, but he who is generous to the needy honors him.

32 The wicked is overthrown through his evildoing, but the righteous finds refuge in his death.

33 Wisdom rests in the heart of a man of understanding, but it makes itself known even in the midst of* fools.

34 Righteousness exalts a nation, but sin is a reproach** to any people.

35 A servant who deals wisely has the king's favor, but his wrath falls on one who acts shamefully.

*   in the midst of ~의 가운데.
** reproach [ripróutʃ] ⑧ 비난하다, 비난의 원인이 되다.

암송 구절 해설

**Whoever despises his neighbor is a sinner,
but blessed is he who is generous to the poor**(14:21).

이웃을 업신여기는 자는 죄를 범하는 자요
빈곤한 자를 불쌍히 여기는 자는 복이 있는 자니라.

가난한 사람은 대체로 보살핌을 받아야 하는 상황에 있지만, 부자들은 다른 이들이 부러워할 만한 재산을 가지고 있습니다. 때문에 부요한 사람은 정작 필요할 때 도움이 되지 않는 친구들에게 둘러싸이기도 합니다. 그 친구들은 부자 친구에게 뭔가를 뜯어낼 궁리를 합니다(참고. 전 5:11). 의인은 이러한 현실의 물결을 거슬러 이웃을 돕습니다. 특히 빈곤한 자를 업신여기는 것이 죄라는 것을 알기 때문에 그들에게 은혜를 베푸는 것입니다. 그러한 사람은 주님의 은혜를 누리게 됩니다.

✏️ 하루 한 문장, 생각 쓰기

오늘 본문을 쓰면서 깨달은 지혜, 새롭게 다짐한 점,
떠오른 생각 등을 자유롭게 적어 보세요.

Proverbs 15

1   A soft answer turns away wrath, but a harsh word stirs up anger.

2   The tongue of the wise commends knowledge, but the mouths of fools pour out folly.

3   The eyes of the LORD are in every place, keeping watch on the evil and the good.

4   A gentle tongue is a tree of life, but perverseness in it breaks the spirit.

5   A fool despises his father's instruction, but whoever heeds* reproof is prudent.

6   In the house of the righteous there is much treasure, but trouble befalls the income of the wicked.

7   The lips of the wise spread knowledge; not so the hearts of fools.

8   The sacrifice of the wicked is an abomination to the LORD, but the prayer of the upright is acceptable to him.

9   The way of the wicked is an abomination to the LORD, but he loves him who pursues righteousness.

10 There is severe discipline for him who forsakes the way; whoever hates reproof will die.

---

*   heed [hiːd] ⑧ 귀 기울이다. 주의하다.

11 Sheol and Abaddon* lie open before the LORD; how much more the hearts of the children of man!

12 A scoffer does not like to be reproved; he will not go to the wise.

13 A glad heart makes a cheerful face, but by sorrow of heart the spirit is crushed.

14 The heart of him who has understanding seeks knowledge, but the mouths of fools feed on folly.

15 All the days of the afflicted** are evil, but the cheerful of heart has a continual feast.

16 Better is a little with the fear of the LORD than great treasure and trouble with it.

17 Better is a dinner of herbs where love is than a fattened ox and hatred with it.

18 A hot-tempered man stirs up strife, but he who is slow to anger quiets contention.

19 The way of a sluggard is like a hedge of thorns, but the path of the upright is a level highway.

20 A wise son makes a glad father, but a foolish man despises his mother.

---

*   Abaddon [əbǽdn] ⑲ 지옥, 나락.

**   afflicted [əflíktid] ⑱ 고통을 받는, 괴로워하는.

21 Folly is a joy to him who lacks sense, but a man of understanding walks straight ahead.

22 Without counsel plans fail, but with many advisers they succeed.

23 To make an apt answer is a joy to a man, and a word in season, how good it is!

24 The path of life leads upward for the prudent, that he may turn away from Sheol beneath.

25 The LORD tears down the house of the proud but maintains the widow's boundaries.

26 The thoughts of the wicked are an abomination to the LORD, but gracious words are pure.

27 Whoever is greedy for* unjust gain troubles his own household, but he who hates bribes** will live.

28 The heart of the righteous ponders how to answer, but the mouth of the wicked pours out evil things.

29 The LORD is far from the wicked, but he hears the prayer of the righteous.

---

*   greedy for ~에 탐욕스러운.

**   bribe [braib] 통 뇌물을 주다, 매수하다.

30 The light of the eyes rejoices the heart, and good news refreshes the bones.

31 The ear that listens to life-giving reproof will dwell among the wise.

32 Whoever ignores instruction despises himself, but he who listens to reproof gains intelligence.

33 The fear of the LORD is instruction in wisdom, and humility comes before honor.

암송 구절 해설

A glad heart makes a cheerful face,
but by sorrow of heart the spirit is crushed(15:13).

마음의 즐거움은 얼굴을 빛나게 하여도
마음의 근심은 심령을 상하게 하느니라.

마음은 사람의 외면과 내면에 영향을 미칩니다. 마음의 즐거움은 빛나는 용모로 나타나는 반면, 마음의 근심은 사람의 기를 꺾고 활력을 서서히 빼앗습니다. 마음의 상태를 보면 그 사람이 어디에서 만족을 얻는지 짐작할 수 있습니다. 마음에 따라 환경을 대하는 태도가 달라지는 것입니다(15절). 가난 혹은 다른 이유로 고난 받는 사람은 일상을 매우 힘겹게 살아가지만, 마음이 즐거운 사람은 하루하루가 축제입니다. 13-15절은 환경이 마음의 태도를 결정한다는 일반적인 전제를 뒤집는 말씀입니다.

오늘 본문을 쓰면서 깨달은 지혜, 새롭게 다짐한 점,
떠오른 생각 등을 자유롭게 적어 보세요.

Proverbs 16

1   The plans of the heart belong to man, but the answer of the tongue is from the LORD.

2   All the ways of a man are pure in his own eyes, but the LORD weighs the spirit.

3   Commit your work to the LORD, and your plans will be established.

4   The LORD has made everything for its purpose, even the wicked for the day of trouble.

5   Everyone who is arrogant* in heart is an abomination to the LORD; be assured, he will not go unpunished.

6   By steadfast love and faithfulness iniquity is atoned for**, and by the fear of the LORD one turns away from evil.

7   When a man's ways please the LORD, he makes even his enemies to be at peace with him.

8   Better is a little with righteousness than great revenues*** with injustice.

9   The heart of man plans his way, but the LORD establishes his steps.

10 An oracle is on the lips of a king; his mouth does not sin in judgment.

---

*   arrogant [ǽrəgənt] ⑱ 거만한, 오만한.

**   atone for ~을 속죄하다.

*** revenue [révənjùː] ⑲ 소득, 수입.

11 A just balance and scales are the LORD's; all the weights in the bag are his work.

12 It is an abomination to kings to do evil, for the throne[*] is established by righteousness.

13 Righteous lips are the delight of a king, and he loves him who speaks what is right.

14 A king's wrath is a messenger of death, and a wise man will appease^{**} it.

15 In the light of a king's face there is life, and his favor is like the clouds that bring the spring rain.

16 How much better to get wisdom than gold! To get understanding is to be chosen rather than silver.

17 The highway of the upright turns aside from evil; whoever guards his way preserves his life.

18 Pride goes before destruction, and a haughty^{***} spirit before a fall.

19 It is better to be of a lowly spirit with the poor than to divide the spoil with the proud.

20 Whoever gives thought to the word will discover good, and blessed is he who trusts in the LORD.

---

* throne [θroun] ⑲ 왕좌, 왕위.
** appease [əpíːz] ⑧ 달래다, 진정시키다, 풀다.
*** haughty [hɔ́ːti] ⑲ 교만한, 오만한, 거만한.

21 The wise of heart is called discerning, and sweetness* of speech increases persuasiveness**.

22 Good sense is a fountain of life to him who has it, but the instruction of fools is folly.

23 The heart of the wise makes his speech judicious and adds persuasiveness to his lips.

24 Gracious words are like a honeycomb, sweetness to the soul and health to the body.

25 There is a way that seems right to a man, but its end is the way to death.

26 A worker's appetite works for him; his mouth urges him on.

27 A worthless man plots evil, and his speech is like a scorching*** fire.

28 A dishonest man spreads strife, and a whisperer separates close friends.

29 A man of violence entices his neighbor and leads him in a way that is not good.

---

*　sweetness [swíːtnis] ⑲ 단맛, 아름다움, 친절.

**　persuasiveness [pərswéisivnis] ⑲ 설득력이 있음.

***　scorching [skɔ́ːrtʃiŋ] ⑲ 맹렬한, 타는 듯한.

30 Whoever winks his eyes plans dishonest things; he who purses his lips brings evil to pass.

31 Gray hair is a crown of glory; it is gained in a righteous life.

32 Whoever is slow to anger is better than the mighty, and he who rules his spirit than he who takes a city.

33 The lot* is cast into the lap, but its every decision is from the LORD.

★   lot [lat] 몡 제비뽑기, 몫, 운 용 나누다, 제비뽑기하다.

암송 구절 해설

The heart of man plans his way,
but the LORD establishes his steps(16:9).

사람이 마음으로 자기의 길을 계획할지라도
그의 걸음을 인도하시는 이는 여호와시니라.

주님은 사람의 걸음을 인도하시는 분입니다. 사람이 계획을 세워도 여호와께서 허락하지 않으시면 그 계획은 시행될 수 없으며, 설령 억지로 일을 진행했다 하더라도 성공하지 못한다는 사실을 늘 기억해야 합니다.

하루 한 문장, 생각 쓰기

오늘 본문을 쓰면서 깨달은 지혜, 새롭게 다짐한 점,
떠오른 생각 등을 자유롭게 적어 보세요.

Proverbs 17

1   Better is a dry morsel* with quiet than a house full of feasting with strife.

2   A servant who deals wisely will rule over a son who acts shamefully and will share the inheritance as one of the brothers.

3   The crucible** is for silver, and the furnace is for gold, and the LORD tests hearts.

4   An evildoer listens to wicked lips, and a liar gives ear to a mischievous tongue.

5   Whoever mocks the poor insults his Maker; he who is glad at calamity will not go unpunished.

6   Grandchildren are the crown of the aged, and the glory of children is their fathers.

7   Fine speech is not becoming to a fool; still less*** is false speech to a prince.

8   A bribe is like a magic stone in the eyes of the one who gives it; wherever he turns he prospers.

9   Whoever covers an offense seeks love, but he who repeats a matter separates close friends.

10 A rebuke goes deeper into a man of understanding than a hundred blows into a fool.

---

*   morsel [mɔ́ːrsəl] 몡 한 조각, 소량.
** crucible [krúːsəbl] 몡 도가니.
*** still less 하물며, 더욱이.

11 An evil man seeks only rebellion*, and a cruel messenger will be sent against him.

12 Let a man meet a she-bear robbed of her cubs rather than a fool in his folly.

13 If anyone returns evil for good, evil will not depart from his house.

14 The beginning of strife is like letting out water, so quit before the quarrel** breaks out***.

15 He who justifies the wicked and he who condemns the righteous are both alike an abomination to the LORD.

16 Why should a fool have money in his hand to buy wisdom when he has no sense?

17 A friend loves at all times, and a brother is born for adversity.

18 One who lacks sense gives a pledge and puts up security in the presence of his neighbor.

19 Whoever loves transgression loves strife; he who makes his door high seeks destruction.

20 A man of crooked heart does not discover good, and one with a dishonest tongue falls into calamity.

---

*   rebellion [ribéljən] ⑲ 반역, 반란, 폭동.

**   quarrel [kwɔ́ːrəl] ⑲ 다툼, 언쟁 ⑤ 다투다, 언쟁하다.

*** break out ~하기 시작하다, 벗어나다, 탈옥하다.

21 He who sires a fool gets himself sorrow, and the father of a fool has no joy.

22 A joyful heart is good medicine, but a crushed spirit dries up the bones.

23 The wicked accepts a bribe in secret to pervert the ways of justice.

24 The discerning sets his face toward wisdom, but the eyes of a fool are on the ends of the earth.

25 A foolish son is a grief to his father and bitterness to her who bore him.

26 To impose a fine on a righteous man is not good, nor to strike the noble for their uprightness.

27 Whoever restrains his words has knowledge, and he who has a cool spirit is a man of understanding.

28 Even a fool who keeps silent is considered wise; when he closes his lips, he is deemed intelligent.

암송 구절 해설

A friend loves at all times,
and a brother is born for adversity(17:17).

친구는 사랑이 끊어지지 아니하고
형제는 위급한 때를 위하여 났느니라.

이 구절을 진짜 위급한 때에는 친구보다 형제를 두는 것이 낫다는 뜻이라고 이해할 수도 있습니다. 그러나 여기에서 말하는 바는 친구든 가족이든 간에 우리를 정말로 사랑하는 사람이라면 어려운 시기를 포함해 언제나 도움이 된다는 것입니다. 참된 사랑은 어려운 상황에 처했다 하더라도 결코 변하지 않습니다.

오늘 본문을 쓰면서 깨달은 지혜, 새롭게 다짐한 점,
떠오른 생각 등을 자유롭게 적어 보세요.

Proverbs 18

1   Whoever isolates* himself seeks his own desire; he breaks out against all sound judgment.

2   A fool takes no pleasure in understanding, but only in expressing his opinion.

3   When wickedness comes, contempt comes also, and with dishonor comes disgrace.

4   The words of a man's mouth are deep waters; the fountain of wisdom is a bubbling brook.

5   It is not good to be partial** to the wicked or to deprive the righteous of justice.

6   A fool's lips walk into a fight, and his mouth invites a beating.

7   A fool's mouth is his ruin, and his lips are a snare to his soul.

8   The words of a whisperer are like delicious morsels; they go down into the inner parts of the body.

9   Whoever is slack in his work is a brother to him who destroys.

10 The name of the LORD is a strong tower; the righteous man runs into*** it and is safe.

---

*   isolate [áisəlèit] ⑧ 분리하다, 고립시키다, 격리하다.
**   partial [pɑ́ːrʃəl] ⑧ 편파적인, 부분적인, 불공평한.
*** run into 뛰어 들어가다, 충돌하다, 우연히 만나다.

11 A rich man's wealth is his strong city, and like a high wall in his imagination.

12 Before destruction a man's heart is haughty, but humility comes before honor.

13 If one gives an answer before he hears, it is his folly and shame.

14 A man's spirit will endure sickness, but a crushed spirit who can bear?

15 An intelligent heart acquires knowledge, and the ear of the wise seeks knowledge.

16 A man's gift makes room for him and brings him before the great.

17 The one who states his case first seems right, until the other comes and examines him.

18 The lot puts an end to quarrels and decides between powerful contenders.

19 A brother offended is more unyielding* than a strong city, and quarreling is like the bars** of a castle.

20 From the fruit of a man's mouth his stomach is satisfied; he is satisfied by the yield of his lips.

---

* unyielding [ənjiːldiŋ] ⑧ 견고한. 단단한.

** bar [baːr] ⑲ 빗장. 막대. 바. 모래톱.

21 Death and life are in the power of the tongue, and those who love it will eat its fruits.

22 He who finds a wife finds a good thing and obtains favor from the LORD.

23 The poor use entreaties, but the rich answer roughly.

24 A man of many companions may come to ruin, but there is a friend who sticks closer than a brother.

암송 구절 해설

**Death and life are in the power of the tongue,
and those who love it will eat its fruits(18:21).**

죽고 사는 것이 혀의 힘에 달렸나니
혀를 쓰기 좋아하는 자는 혀의 열매를 먹으리라.

사람의 말은 자신에게로 되돌아옵니다. 따라서 우리는 자신이 한 말과 그 결과들을 먹고 산다고 해도 과언이 아닙니다. 21절은 미련한 사람이 자기의 미련한 말과 그 결과를 맛보게 될 것이라는 사실을 암시합니다. 혀에는 '죽음'과 '삶'을 초래하는 힘이 있습니다. 선을 위해서든 악을 위해서든 혀를 쓰기 좋아하는 자는 혀의 열매를 먹게 될 것입니다. 따라서 자신이 하는 말의 결과로 살기도 하고 죽기도 한다는 사실을 기억하며 말하는 데 신중을 기해야 합니다.

오늘 본문을 쓰면서 깨달은 지혜, 새롭게 다짐한 점,
떠오른 생각 등을 자유롭게 적어 보세요.

Proverbs 19

1 Better is a poor person who walks in his integrity than one who is crooked in speech and is a fool.

2 Desire without knowledge is not good, and whoever makes haste with his feet misses his way.

3 When a man's folly brings his way to ruin, his heart rages* against the LORD.

4 Wealth brings many new friends, but a poor man is deserted by his friend.

5 A false witness will not go unpunished, and he who breathes out lies will not escape.

6 Many seek the favor of a generous man, and everyone is a friend to a man who gives gifts.

7 All a poor man's brothers hate him; how much more do his friends go far from him! He pursues them with words, but does not have them.

8 Whoever gets sense loves his own soul; he who keeps understanding will discover good.

9 A false witness will not go unpunished, and he who breathes out lies will perish.

10 It is not fitting for a fool to live in luxury, much less for a slave to rule over princes.

---

* rage [reidʒ] ⑱ 분노, 격분, 맹렬함.

11 Good sense makes one slow to anger, and it is his glory to overlook an offense.

12 A king's wrath is like the growling* of a lion, but his favor is like dew on the grass.

13 A foolish son is ruin to his father, and a wife's quarreling is a continual dripping of rain.

14 House and wealth are inherited from fathers, but a prudent wife is from the LORD.

15 Slothfulness casts into a deep sleep, and an idle** person will suffer hunger.

16 Whoever keeps the commandment keeps his life; he who despises his ways will die.

17 Whoever is generous to the poor lends to the LORD, and he will repay him for his deed.

18 Discipline your son, for there is hope; do not set your heart on putting him to death.

19 A man of great wrath will pay the penalty, for if you deliver him, you will only have to do it again.

20 Listen to advice and accept instruction, that you may gain wisdom in the future.

21 Many are the plans in the mind of a man, but it is the purpose of the LORD that will stand.

---

* growling [gráuliŋ] ⑱ 으르렁거리는.
** idle [áidl] ⑱ 일하지 않는, 나태한, 한가한.

22 What is desired in a man is steadfast love, and a poor man is better than a liar.

23 The fear of the LORD leads to life, and whoever has it rests satisfied; he will not be visited by harm.

24 The sluggard buries his hand in the dish and will not even bring it back to his mouth.

25 Strike a scoffer, and the simple will learn prudence; reprove a man of understanding, and he will gain knowledge.

26 He who does violence to his father and chases away his mother is a son who brings shame and reproach.

27 Cease to hear instruction, my son, and you will stray from the words of knowledge.

28 A worthless witness mocks at justice, and the mouth of the wicked devours iniquity.

29 Condemnation* is ready for scoffers, and beating for the backs of fools.

---

* condemnation [kàndemnéiʃən] 몡 유죄 선고, 심한 비난.

암송 구절 해설

**What is desired in a man is steadfast love,
and a poor man is better than a liar**(19:22).

사람은 자기의 인자함으로 남에게 사모함을 받느니라
가난한 자는 거짓말하는 자보다 나으니라.

여기에서 인자함은 단순히 인간의 친절함보다는 주님의 특징인 성실한 사랑을 뜻한다고 볼 수 있습니다. 사람들은 성실함을 존중합니다. 그것은 부귀보다 사모하고 존중할 만한 가치입니다. 그렇기 때문에 가난한 자가 거짓말하는 불성실한 자보다 나은 것입니다.

✎ 하루 한 문장, 생각 쓰기

오늘 본문을 쓰면서 깨달은 지혜, 새롭게 다짐한 점,
떠오른 생각 등을 자유롭게 적어 보세요.

Proverbs 20

1   Wine is a mocker, strong drink a brawler, and whoever is led astray by it is not wise.

2   The terror of a king is like the growling of a lion; whoever provokes him to anger forfeits* his life.

3   It is an honor for a man to keep aloof from strife, but every fool will be quarreling.

4   The sluggard does not plow in the autumn; he will seek at harvest and have nothing.

5   The purpose in a man's heart is like deep water, but a man of understanding will draw it out.

6   Many a man proclaims his own steadfast love, but a faithful man who can find?

7   The righteous who walks in his integrity—blessed are his children after him!

8   A king who sits on the throne of judgment winnows all evil with his eyes.

9   Who can say, "I have made my heart pure; I am clean from my sin"?

10   Unequal weights and unequal measures are both alike an abomination to the LORD.

11   Even a child makes himself known by his acts, by whether his conduct is pure and upright.

---

*   forfeit [fɔ́ːrfit] ⑧ 상실하다 ⑨ 벌금, 몰수.

12 The hearing ear and the seeing eye, the LORD has made them both.

13 Love not sleep, lest you come to poverty; open your eyes, and you will have plenty of bread.

14 "Bad, bad," says the buyer, but when he goes away, then he boasts.

15 There is gold and abundance of costly* stones, but the lips of knowledge are a precious jewel.

16 Take a man's garment** when he has put up security for a stranger, and hold it in pledge when he puts up security for foreigners.

17 Bread gained by deceit is sweet to a man, but afterward his mouth will be full of gravel***.

18 Plans are established by counsel; by wise guidance wage war.

19 Whoever goes about slandering reveals secrets; therefore do not associate with a simple babbler.

20 If one curses his father or his mother, his lamp will be put out in utter darkness.

21 An inheritance gained hastily in the beginning will not be blessed in the end.

22 Do not say, "I will repay evil"; wait for the LORD, and he will deliver you.

---

*   costly [kɔ́:stli] ⑬ 값비싼, 사치스러운.

**   garment [gάːrmənt] ⑲ 의류, 덮개 ⑧ 입히다. 씌우다.

*** gravel [grǽvəl] ⑲ 자갈 ⑧ 어리둥절하게 하다.

23 Unequal weights are an abomination to the LORD, and false scales are not good.

24 A man's steps are from the LORD; how then can man understand his way?

25 It is a snare to say rashly, "It is holy," and to reflect only after making vows.

26 A wise king winnows* the wicked and drives the wheel over them.

27 The spirit of man is the lamp of the LORD, searching all his innermost** parts.

28 Steadfast love and faithfulness preserve the king, and by steadfast love his throne is upheld.

29 The glory of young men is their strength, but the splendor of old men is their gray hair.

30 Blows that wound cleanse away evil; strokes make clean the innermost parts.

---

* winnow [wínou] ⑧ 키질하다. 까부르다.

** innermost [inərmoust] ⑲ 가장 깊은, 맨 안쪽의.

암송 구절 해설

Do not say, "I will repay evil"; wait for the LORD,
and he will deliver you(20:22).

너는 악을 갚겠다 말하지 말고 여호와를 기다리라
그가 너를 구원하시리라.

그리스도인은 하나님이 악을 바로잡아 주시기를 바라며 인내해야 합니다. 아무리 억울한 일을 당했다 할지라도 직접 복수하기보다는 주님을 의지하고 기다리는 것이 훨씬 낫습니다. 주님이 개입하셔서 기다린 자를 구원하실 것이기 때문입니다. 주님은 피해자를 돌보시고 가해자를 심판하실 것입니다.

오늘 본문을 쓰면서 깨달은 지혜, 새롭게 다짐한 점.
떠오른 생각 등을 자유롭게 적어 보세요.

Proverbs 21

1   The king's heart is a stream of water in the hand of the LORD; he turns it wherever he will.

2   Every way of a man is right in his own eyes, but the LORD weighs the heart.

3   To do righteousness and justice is more acceptable to the LORD than sacrifice.

4   Haughty eyes and a proud heart, the lamp of the wicked, are sin.

5   The plans of the diligent lead surely to abundance, but everyone who is hasty comes only to poverty.

6   The getting of treasures by a lying tongue is a fleeting vapor* and a snare of death.

7   The violence of the wicked will sweep them away, because they refuse to do what is just.

8   The way of the guilty is crooked, but the conduct of the pure is upright.

9   It is better to live in a corner of the housetop than in a house shared with a quarrelsome** wife.

10   The soul of the wicked desires evil; his neighbor finds no mercy in his eyes.

11   When a scoffer is punished, the simple becomes wise; when a wise man is instructed, he gains knowledge.

---

*   vapor [véipər] ⑲ 안개, 증기 ⑧ 증발하다.
**   quarrelsome [kwɔ́:rəlsəm] ⑲ 다투기 좋아하는, 성급한.

12 The Righteous One observes the house of the wicked; he throws the wicked down to ruin.

13 Whoever closes his ear to the cry of the poor will himself call out and not be answered.

14 A gift in secret averts* anger, and a concealed bribe, strong wrath.

15 When justice is done, it is a joy to the righteous but terror to evildoers.

16 One who wanders from the way of good sense will rest in the assembly of the dead.

17 Whoever loves pleasure will be a poor man; he who loves wine and oil will not be rich.

18 The wicked is a ransom for the righteous, and the traitor for the upright.

19 It is better to live in a desert land than with a quarrelsome and fretful** woman.

20 Precious treasure and oil are in a wise man's dwelling, but a foolish man devours it.

21 Whoever pursues righteousness and kindness will find life, righteousness, and honor.

22 A wise man scales the city of the mighty and brings down the stronghold in which they trust.

---

*   avert [əvə́:rt] ⑤ 피하다, 막다.

**   fretful [frétfəl] ⑧ 안달하는, 초조해하는, 조급한.

23 Whoever keeps his mouth and his tongue keeps himself out of trouble.

24 "Scoffer" is the name of the arrogant, haughty man who acts with arrogant pride.

25 The desire of the sluggard kills him, for his hands refuse to labor.

26 All day long he craves and craves, but the righteous gives and does not hold back.

27 The sacrifice of the wicked is an abomination; how much more when he brings it with evil intent.

28 A false witness will perish, but the word of a man who hears will endure.

29 A wicked man puts on a bold face, but the upright gives thought to his ways.

30 No wisdom, no understanding, no counsel can avail against the LORD.

31 The horse is made ready for the day of battle, but the victory belongs to* the LORD.

---

*   belong to ~의 것이다, ~에 속하다.

암송 구절 해설

Every way of a man is right in his own eyes,
but the LORD weighs the heart(21:2).

사람의 행위가 자기 보기에는 모두 정직하여도
여호와는 마음을 감찰하시느니라.

사람들은 스스로를 기만하거나 하나님의 도덕 질서를 뒤집으면서도 자신의 행위가 정직하다고 잘못 판단하기도 합니다. 중요한 것은 주님이 인간의 마음을 정확히 판단하신다는 사실입니다. 따라서 지혜로운 자는 주권자이신 주님의 평가에 가장 먼저 관심을 기울입니다.

오늘 본문을 쓰면서 깨달은 지혜, 새롭게 다짐한 점.
떠오른 생각 등을 자유롭게 적어 보세요.

Proverbs 22

1   A good name is to be chosen rather than great riches, and favor is better than silver or gold.

2   The rich and the poor meet together; the LORD is the Maker of them all.

3   The prudent sees danger and hides himself, but the simple go on and suffer for it.

4   The reward for humility and fear of the LORD is riches and honor and life.

5   Thorns* and snares are in the way of the crooked; whoever guards his soul will keep far from them.

6   Train up a child in the way he should go; even when he is old he will not depart from it.

7   The rich rules over the poor, and the borrower** is the slave of the lender.

8   Whoever sows injustice will reap calamity, and the rod of his fury will fail.

9   Whoever has a bountiful eye will be blessed, for he shares his bread with the poor.

10   Drive out a scoffer, and strife will go out, and quarreling and abuse will cease.

11   He who loves purity of heart, and whose speech is gracious, will have the king as his friend.

---

*   thorn [θɔːrn] ⑲ 가시.
*   borrower [bɑ́rouər] ⑲ 빚진 사람, 표절자.

12 The eyes of the LORD keep watch over knowledge, but he overthrows the words of the traitor.

13 The sluggard says, "There is a lion outside! I shall be killed in the streets!"

14 The mouth of forbidden women is a deep pit; he with whom the LORD is angry will fall into* it.

15 Folly is bound up in the heart of a child, but the rod of discipline drives it far from him.

16 Whoever oppresses the poor to increase his own wealth, or gives to the rich, will only come to poverty.

Words of the Wise

17 Incline your ear, and hear the words of the wise, and apply your heart to my knowledge,

18 for it will be pleasant if you keep them within you, if all of them are ready on your lips.

19 That your trust may be in the LORD, I have made them known to you today, even to you.

20 Have I not written for you thirty sayings of counsel and knowledge,

21 to make you know what is right and true, that you may give a true answer to those who sent you?

---

* fall into ～에 빠지다, 빠져들다.

22 Do not rob the poor, because he is poor, or crush the afflicted at the gate,

23 for the LORD will plead their cause and rob of life those who rob them.

24 Make no friendship with a man given to anger, nor go with a wrathful man,

25 lest you learn his ways and entangle yourself in a snare.

26 Be not one of those who give pledges, who put up security for debts*.

27 If you have nothing with which to pay, why should your bed be taken from under you?

28 Do not move the ancient landmark that your fathers have set.

29 Do you see a man skillful in his work? He will stand before kings; he will not stand before obscure** men.

---

*   debt [det] ⑱ 빚, 부채.

** obscure [əbskjúər] ⑲ 불분명한, 무명의, 애매한.

암송 구절 해설

A good name is to be chosen rather than great riches,
and favor is better than silver or gold(22:1).

많은 재물보다 명예를 택할 것이요
은이나 금보다 은총을 더욱 택할 것이니라.

좋은 평판(명예, 은총)은 많은 재물보다 더 가치가 있습니다. 부만으로는 좋은 평판을 얻을 수 없습니다. 그러므로 평판보다 부를 높이 평가해서는 안 됩니다. 그렇다면 어떻게 좋은 평판을 얻을 수 있을까요? 바로 지혜를 통해 얻을 수 있습니다. 또한 지혜는 부를 덤으로 줄 수도 있습니다. 그러므로 부를 택하기보다 지혜를 통해 좋은 평판을 얻는 데 힘을 쏟아야 합니다.

오늘 본문을 쓰면서 깨달은 지혜, 새롭게 다짐한 점,
떠오른 생각 등을 자유롭게 적어 보세요.

Proverbs 23

1 When you sit down to eat with a ruler, observe carefully what is before you,

2 and put a knife to your throat if you are given to appetite.

3 Do not desire his delicacies*, for they are deceptive food.

4 Do not toil to acquire wealth; be discerning enough to desist**.

5 When your eyes light on it, it is gone, for suddenly it sprouts wings, flying like an eagle toward heaven.

6 Do not eat the bread of a man who is stingy***; do not desire his delicacies,

7 for he is like one who is inwardly calculating. "Eat and drink!" he says to you, but his heart is not with you.

8 You will vomit up the morsels that you have eaten, and waste your pleasant words.

9 Do not speak in the hearing of a fool, for he will despise the good sense of your words.

10 Do not move an ancient landmark or enter the fields of the fatherless,

11 for their Redeemer is strong; he will plead their cause against you.

12 Apply your heart to instruction and your ear to words of knowledge.

---

* delicacy [délikəsi] 명 별미, 섬세함, 미묘함.

** desist [dizíst] 동 그만두다.

*** stingy [stíndʒi] 형 인색한, 부족한, 찌르는.

13 Do not withhold discipline from a child; if you strike him with a rod, he will not die.

14 If you strike him with the rod, you will save his soul from Sheol.

15 My son, if your heart is wise, my heart too will be glad.

16 My inmost being will exult when your lips speak what is right.

17 Let not your heart envy sinners, but continue in the fear of the LORD all the day.

18 Surely there is a future, and your hope will not be cut off.

19 Hear, my son, and be wise, and direct your heart in the way.

20 Be not among drunkards* or among gluttonous** eaters of meat,

21 for the drunkard and the glutton will come to poverty, and slumber will clothe them with rags.

22 Listen to your father who gave you life, and do not despise your mother when she is old.

23 Buy truth, and do not sell it; buy wisdom, instruction, and understanding.

24 The father of the righteous will greatly rejoice; he who fathers a wise son will be glad in him.

---

* drunkard [drʌŋkərd] ⑲ 술주정뱅이, 술고래.

** gluttonous [glʌtənəs] ⑲ 탐욕스러운, 많이 먹는.

25 Let your father and mother be glad; let her who bore you rejoice.

26 My son, give me your heart, and let your eyes observe my ways.

27 For a prostitute is a deep pit; an adulteress is a narrow well.

28 She lies in wait like a robber and increases the traitors among mankind.

29 Who has woe? Who has sorrow? Who has strife? Who has complaining? Who has wounds without cause? Who has redness of eyes?

30 Those who tarry long over wine; those who go to try mixed wine.

31 Do not look at wine when it is red, when it sparkles in the cup and goes down smoothly.

32 In the end it bites like a serpent and stings like an adder.

33 Your eyes will see strange things, and your heart utter perverse things.

34 You will be like one who lies down in the midst of the sea, like one who lies on the top of a mast.

35 "They struck me," you will say, "but I was not hurt; they beat me, but I did not feel it. When shall I awake? I must have another drink."

암송 구절 해설

Let not your heart envy sinners,
but continue in the fear of the LORD all the day(23:17).

네 마음으로 죄인의 형통을 부러워하지 말고
항상 여호와를 경외하라.

지혜로운 사람은 죄인이 잠시 형통하는 것처럼 보여도 마음으로 죄인을 부러워하지 않을 것입니다. 오히려 하늘을 우러러보면서 항상 여호와를 경외하기를 열망할 것입니다. 또한 지혜로운 사람은 앞을 보면서 자신이 그런 열망을 품는 데에는 나름의 이유가 있음을 깨달을 것입니다. 멸망에 직면하는 악인들과 달리 주님을 경외하는 이들에게는 끊어지지 않을 소망, 즉 영생이 있기 때문입니다(18절).

✏️ 하루 한 문장, 생각 쓰기

오늘 본문을 쓰면서 깨달은 지혜, 새롭게 다짐한 점,
떠오른 생각 등을 자유롭게 적어 보세요.

DATE. . . .

Proverbs 24

1   Be not envious of evil men, nor desire to be with them,

2   for their hearts devise violence, and their lips talk of trouble.

3   By wisdom a house is built, and by understanding it is established;

4   by knowledge the rooms are filled with all precious and pleasant riches.

5   A wise man is full of strength, and a man of knowledge enhances* his might,

6   for by wise guidance you can wage your war, and in abundance of coun selors there is victory.

7   Wisdom is too high for a fool; in the gate he does not open his mouth.

8   Whoever plans to do evil will be called a schemer**.

9   The devising of folly is sin, and the scoffer is an abomination to mankind.

10 If you faint in the day of adversity, your strength is small.

11 Rescue*** those who are being taken away to death; hold back those who are stumbling to the slaughter.

---

*   enhance [inhǽns] ⑧ 더하다, 향상하다, 강화하다.

**   schemer [skí:mər] ⑨ 모사꾼, 책략가.

*** rescue [réskju:] ⑧ 구조하다, 해방시키다.

12 If you say, "Behold, we did not know this," does not he who weighs the heart perceive it? Does not he who keeps watch over your soul know it, and will he not repay man according to his work?

13 My son, eat honey, for it is good, and the drippings of the honeycomb are sweet to your taste.

14 Know that wisdom is such to your soul; if you find it, there will be a future, and your hope will not be cut off.

15 Lie not in wait as a wicked man against the dwelling of the righteous; do no violence to his home;

16 for the righteous falls seven times and rises again, but the wicked stumble in times of calamity.

17 Do not rejoice when your enemy falls, and let not your heart be glad when he stumbles,

18 lest the LORD see it and be displeased, and turn away his anger from him.

19 Fret* not yourself because of evildoers, and be not envious of the wicked,

20 for the evil man has no future; the lamp of the wicked will be put out.

21 My son, fear the LORD and the king, and do not join with those who do otherwise,

---

* fret [fret] ⑧ 초초해하다, 애타다 ⑲ 초조, 불안.

22 for disaster will arise suddenly from them, and who knows the ruin that will come from them both?

More Sayings of the Wise

23 These also are sayings of the wise. Partiality* in judging is not good.

24 Whoever says to the wicked, "You are in the right," will be cursed by peoples, abhorred** by nations,

25 but those who rebuke the wicked will have delight, and a good blessing will come upon them.

26 Whoever gives an honest answer kisses the lips.

27 Prepare your work outside; get everything ready for yourself in the field, and after that build your house.

28 Be not a witness against your neighbor without cause, and do not deceive with your lips.

29 Do not say, "I will do to him as he has done to me; I will pay the man back for what he has done."

---

* partiality [pɑ̀ːrʃiǽləti] ⑱ 편애. 편파. 불공평.

** abhor [æbhɔ́ːr] ⑧ 혐오하다. 증오하다.

30 I passed by the field of a sluggard, by the vineyard* of a man lacking sense,

31 and behold, it was all overgrown with thorns; the ground was covered with nettles**, and its stone wall was broken down.

32 Then I saw and considered it; I looked and received instruction.

33 A little sleep, a little slumber, a little folding of the hands to rest,

34 and poverty will come upon you like a robber, and want like an armed man.

---

*   vineyard [vínjərd] ⑲ 포도원.

**   nettle [nétl] ⑲ 쐐기풀 ⑧ 화나게 하다, 찌르다.

암송 구절 해설

Prepare your work outside; get everything ready for yourself in the field, and after that build your house(24:27).

네 일을 밖에서 다스리며 너를 위하여 밭에서 준비하고
그 후에 네 집을 세울지니라.

이 말씀은 '중요한 일부터 먼저 하라'는 뜻과 같습니다. 지혜로운 사람이라면 먼저 밖의 일에 주의를 기울이고 그런 다음 자기 집을 세울 것입니다. 농업과 관련지어 말하면, 자기 밭을 마련하여 그 농작물로 가족을 부양하는 것을 의미합니다. 더 넓게 말하면, 지혜로운 사람은 적절한 준비 없이 어떤 일을 시작하지 않는다는 뜻입니다.

오늘 본문을 쓰면서 깨달은 지혜, 새롭게 다짐한 점,
떠오른 생각 등을 자유롭게 적어 보세요.

Proverbs 25

More Proverbs of Solomon

1 These also are proverbs of Solomon which the men of Hezekiah king of Judah copied.

2 It is the glory of God to conceal things, but the glory of kings is to search things out.

3 As the heavens for height, and the earth for depth, so the heart of kings is unsearchable.

4 Take away the dross* from the silver, and the smith has material for a vessel**;

5 take away the wicked from the presence of the king, and his throne will be established in righteousness.

6 Do not put yourself forward in the king's presence or stand in the place of the great,

7 for it is better to be told, "Come up here," than to be put lower in the presence of a noble.

What your eyes have seen

8 do not hastily bring into court, for what will you do in the end, when your neighbor puts you to shame?

9 Argue your case with your neighbor himself, and do not reveal another's secret,

---

* dross [drɔːs] ⑲ 찌꺼기, 불순물.

** vessel [vésəl] ⑲ 그릇, 배, 혈관.

10 lest he who hears you bring shame upon you, and your ill repute have no end.

11 A word fitly* spoken is like apples of gold in a setting of silver.

12 Like a gold ring or an ornament of gold is a wise reprover to a listening ear.

13 Like the cold of snow in the time of harvest is a faithful messenger to those who send him; he refreshes the soul of his masters.

14 Like clouds and wind without rain is a man who boasts of a gift he does not give.

15 With patience a ruler may be persuaded, and a soft tongue will break a bone.

16 If you have found honey, eat only enough for you, lest you have your fill of it and vomit** it.

17 Let your foot be seldom in your neighbor's house, lest he have his fill of you and hate you.

18 A man who bears false witness against his neighbor is like a war club, or a sword, or a sharp arrow.

19 Trusting in a treacherous man in time of trouble is like a bad tooth or a foot that slips.

20 Whoever sings songs to a heavy heart is like one who takes off a garment on a cold day, and like vinegar on soda***.

---

* fitly [fítli] ⑨ 알맞게, 합당한.

** vomit [vάmit] ⑧ 토하다, 게우다 ⑲ 구토.

*** soda [sóudə] ⑲ 소다, 탄산수, 소다수.

21 If your enemy is hungry, give him bread to eat, and if he is thirsty, give him water to drink,

22 for you will heap burning coals on his head, and the LORD will reward you.

23 The north wind brings forth rain, and a backbiting tongue, angry looks.

24 It is better to live in a corner of the housetop than in a house shared with a quarrelsome wife.

25 Like cold water to a thirsty soul, so is good news from a far country.

26 Like a muddied spring or a polluted* fountain is a righteous man who gives way before the wicked.

27 It is not good to eat much honey, nor is it glorious to seek one's own glory.

28 A man without self-control is like a city broken into and left without walls.

---

* polluted [pəlúːtid] 형 타락한, 오염된.

암송 구절 해설

**With patience a ruler may be persuaded,
and a soft tongue will break a bone(25:15).**

오래 참으면 관원도 설득할 수 있나니
부드러운 혀는 뼈를 꺾느니라.

많은 사람이 뼈처럼 딱딱하고 완고한 관원들을 상대하려면 그들과 똑같이 강경하게 나가는 것이 최선의 방법이라고 생각합니다. 그러나 가장 좋은 접근법은 오래 참음, 곧 인내입니다. 지혜롭고, 끈기 있고, 부드러운 말은 강경한 자들에게 파고들어 그들을 설득합니다. 지혜로운 사람은 끈기 있고 개방적이며, 따스한 성격을 통해 그리고 민감하고 재치 있는 말을 통해 자신의 생각을 다른 이에게 전할 수 있습니다.

오늘 본문을 쓰면서 깨달은 지혜, 새롭게 다짐한 점.
떠오른 생각 등을 자유롭게 적어 보세요.

Proverbs 26

1 Like snow in summer or rain in harvest, so honor is not fitting for a fool.

2 Like a sparrow in its flitting*, like a swallow in its flying, a curse that is causeless does not alight.

3 A whip for the horse, a bridle for the donkey, and a rod for the back of fools.

4 Answer not a fool according to his folly, lest you be like him yourself.

5 Answer a fool according to his folly, lest he be wise in his own eyes.

6 Whoever sends a message by the hand of a fool cuts off his own feet and drinks violence.

7 Like a lame** man's legs, which hang useless, is a proverb in the mouth of fools.

8 Like one who binds the stone in the sling is one who gives honor to a fool.

9 Like a thorn that goes up into the hand of a drunkard is a proverb in the mouth of fools.

10 Like an archer who wounds everyone is one who hires a passing fool or drunkard.

---

*   flitting [flítiŋ] ⑱ 빨리 지나가는 ⑲ 야반도주.

** lame [leim] ⑱ 다리를 저는, 서투른.

11 Like a dog that returns to his vomit is a fool who repeats his folly.

12 Do you see a man who is wise in his own eyes? There is more hope for a fool than for him.

13 The sluggard says, "There is a lion in the road! There is a lion in the streets!"

14 As a door turns on its hinges*, so does a sluggard on his bed.

15 The sluggard buries his hand in the dish; it wears him out to bring it back to his mouth.

16 The sluggard is wiser in his own eyes than seven men who can answer sensibly.

17 Whoever meddles in a quarrel not his own is like one who takes a passing dog by the ears.

18 Like a madman who throws firebrands**, arrows, and death

19 is the man who deceives his neighbor and says, "I am only joking!"

20 For lack of wood the fire goes out, and where there is no whisperer, quarreling ceases.

---

*   hinge [hindʒ] ⑲ 돌쩌귀, 경첩.

** firebrand [faiərbrænd] ⑲ 햇불, 선동가.

21 As charcoal to hot embers and wood to fire, so is a quarrelsome man for kindling strife.

22 The words of a whisperer are like delicious morsels; they go down into the inner parts of the body.

23 Like the glaze covering an earthen vessel are fervent lips with an evil heart.

24 Whoever hates disguises himself with his lips and harbors deceit in his heart;

25 when he speaks graciously, believe him not, for there are seven abominations in his heart;

26 though his hatred be covered with deception, his wickedness will be exposed in the assembly.

27 Whoever digs a pit will fall into it, and a stone will come back on him who starts it rolling.

28 A lying tongue hates its victims, and a flattering mouth works ruin.

암송 구절 해설

**Do you see a man who is wise in his own eyes?
There is more hope for a fool than for him(26:12).**

네가 스스로 지혜롭게 여기는 자를 보느냐
그보다 미련한 자에게 오히려 희망이 있느니라.

스스로 지혜롭게 여기는 사람은 미련한 사람보다 더 대화하기가 어렵고 성장 가능성이 낮습니다. 그는 자신의 명철을 의지하기 때문에(참고. 3:5) 자신이 지혜에 도달한 것을 자랑스럽게 여기며 더 이상의 교훈이 필요 없다고 생각하기 때문입니다. 미련한 자에게 희망이 있는 까닭은 그가 적어도 모종의 징계에 응답할 줄 알기 때문입니다. 결국 스스로 지혜롭다고 여기는 사람은 "나는 지혜롭다"라고 말하자마자 미련한 자보다 더 미련하게 되고 말 것입니다.

오늘 본문을 쓰면서 깨달은 지혜, 새롭게 다짐한 점,
떠오른 생각 등을 자유롭게 적어 보세요.

Proverbs 27

1　Do not boast about tomorrow, for you do not know what a day may bring.

2　Let another praise you, and not your own mouth; a stranger, and not your own lips.

3　A stone is heavy, and sand is weighty, but a fool's provocation* is heavier than both.

4　Wrath is cruel, anger is overwhelming**, but who can stand before jealousy?

5　Better is open rebuke than hidden love.

6　Faithful are the wounds of a friend; profuse are the kisses of an enemy.

7　One who is full loathes honey, but to one who is hungry everything bitter is sweet.

8　Like a bird that strays from its nest is a man who strays from*** his home.

9　Oil and perfume make the heart glad, and the sweetness of a friend comes from his earnest counsel.

10　Do not forsake your friend and your father's friend, and do not go to your brother's house in the day of your calamity. Better is a neighbor who is near than a brother who is far away.

---

*　provocation [prɑ̀vəkéiʃən] 圕 분개, 도발, 자극.
**　overwhelming [òuvərhwélmiŋ] 圕 압도적인, 굉장한.
***　stray from ~에서 빗나가다, ~에서 벗어나다.

11 Be wise, my son, and make my heart glad, that I may answer him who reproaches me.

12 The prudent sees danger and hides himself, but the simple go on and suffer for it.

13 Take a man's garment when he has put up security for a stranger, and hold it in pledge when he puts up security for an adulteress.

14 Whoever blesses his neighbor with a loud voice, rising early in the morning, will be counted as cursing.

15 A continual dripping on a rainy day and a quarrelsome wife are alike;

16 to restrain her is to restrain* the wind or to grasp oil in one's right hand.

17 Iron sharpens iron, and one man sharpens another.

18 Whoever tends a fig tree will eat its fruit, and he who guards his master will be honored.

19 As in water face reflects** face, so the heart of man reflects the man.

20 Sheol and Abaddon are never satisfied, and never satisfied are the eyes of man.

---

*   restrain [ristréin] ⑧ 제어하다, 억제하다, 구속하다.

**   reflect [riflékt] ⑧ 반사하다, 반영하다, 보여주다.

21 The crucible is for silver, and the furnace is for gold, and a man is tested by his praise.

22 Crush a fool in a mortar* with a pestle** along with crushed grain, yet his folly will not depart from him.

23 Know well the condition of your flocks, and give attention to your herds,

24 for riches do not last forever; and does a crown endure to all generations?

25 When the grass is gone and the new growth appears and the vegetation*** of the mountains is gathered,

26 the lambs will provide your clothing, and the goats the price of a field.

27 There will be enough goats' milk for your food, for the food of your household and maintenance for your girls.

---

*   mortar [mɔ́:rtər] ⑲ 절구, 막자사발, 박격포.

**   pestle [pésl] ⑲ 절굿공이.

*** vegetation [vèdʒətéiʃən] ⑲ 초목.

암송 구절 해설

**Do not boast about tomorrow,
for you do not know what a day may bring(27:1).**

너는 내일 일을 자랑하지 말라 하루 동안에
무슨 일이 일어날지 네가 알 수 없음이니라.

지혜로운 사람은 아직 이루어지지 않은 일에 대해 자랑하지 않습니다. 내일 무슨 일이 일어날지는 누구도 확실히 알 수 없기 때문입니다. 현재와 미래는 하나님의 손안에 있는 까닭에 지혜로운 자는 주님을 경외하면서 계획을 세우고 그분의 처분을 겸손히 신뢰합니다.

✎ 하루 한 문장, 생각 쓰기

오늘 본문을 쓰면서 깨달은 지혜, 새롭게 다짐한 점,
떠오른 생각 등을 자유롭게 적어 보세요.

Proverbs 28

1 The wicked flee when no one pursues, but the righteous are bold as a lion.

2 When a land transgresses*, it has many rulers, but with a man of understanding and knowledge, its stability** will long continue.

3 A poor man who oppresses the poor is a beating rain that leaves no food.

4 Those who forsake the law praise the wicked, but those who keep the law strive against them.

5 Evil men do not understand justice, but those who seek the LORD understand it completely.

6 Better is a poor man who walks in his integrity than a rich man who is crooked in his ways.

7 The one who keeps the law is a son with understanding, but a companion of gluttons shames his father.

8 Whoever multiplies his wealth by interest and profit gathers it for him who is generous to the poor.

9 If one turns away his ear from hearing the law, even his prayer is an abomination.

10 Whoever misleads the upright into an evil way will fall into his own pit, but the blameless will have a goodly inheritance.

---

*   transgress [trænsgrés] ⑧ 넘다. 위반하다.

**   stability [stəbíləti] ⑲ 안정, 지속.

11 A rich man is wise in his own eyes, but a poor man who has understanding will find him out.

12 When the righteous triumph, there is great glory, but when the wicked rise, people hide themselves.

13 Whoever conceals his transgressions will not prosper, but he who confesses and forsakes them will obtain mercy.

14 Blessed is the one who fears the LORD always, but whoever hardens his heart will fall into calamity.

15 Like a roaring lion or a charging bear is a wicked ruler over a poor people.

16 A ruler who lacks understanding is a cruel oppressor, but he who hates unjust gain will prolong his days.

17 If one is burdened with the blood of another, he will be a fugitive* until death; let no one help him.

18 Whoever walks in integrity will be delivered, but he who is crooked in his ways will suddenly fall.

19 Whoever works his land will have plenty of bread, but he who follows worthless pursuits will have plenty of poverty.

20 A faithful man will abound with blessings, but whoever hastens to be rich will not go unpunished.

---

*   fugitive [fjúːdʒətiv] ⑲ 도망자 ⑲ 도망친. 일시적인.

21 To show partiality is not good, but for a piece of bread a man will do wrong.

22 A stingy man hastens after wealth and does not know that poverty will come upon him.

23 Whoever rebukes a man will afterward find more favor than he who flatters with his tongue.

24 Whoever robs his father or his mother and says, "That is no transgression," is a companion to a man who destroys.

25 A greedy man stirs up strife, but the one who trusts in the LORD will be enriched.

26 Whoever trusts in his own mind is a fool, but he who walks in wisdom will be delivered.

27 Whoever gives to the poor will not want, but he who hides his eyes will get many a curse.

28 When the wicked rise, people hide themselves, but when they perish, the righteous increase.

암송 구절 해설

**Whoever conceals his transgressions will not prosper,
but he who confesses and forsakes them will obtain mercy(28:13).**

자기의 죄를 숨기는 자는 형통하지 못하나 죄를 자복하고
버리는 자는 불쌍히 여김을 받으리라.

대부분의 사람은 자기의 죄를 숨기려는 경향이 있습니다. 하지만 그런 길을 계속해서 간다면 형통하지 못할 것입니다. 죄를 진실로 뉘우치는 것이 더 나은 길입니다. 죄를 자복하는 일에는 하나님을 찬미하고 하나님의 위대하심, 하나님의 정의, 하나님의 은혜를 인정하는 일이 수반됩니다.

✎ 하루 한 문장, 생각 쓰기

오늘 본문을 쓰면서 깨달은 지혜, 새롭게 다짐한 점,
떠오른 생각 등을 자유롭게 적어 보세요.

DATE. . . .

Proverbs 29

1 He who is often reproved, yet stiffens his neck, will suddenly be broken beyond healing.

2 When the righteous increase, the people rejoice, but when the wicked rule, the people groan.

3 He who loves wisdom makes his father glad, but a companion of prostitutes squanders* his wealth.

4 By justice a king builds up the land, but he who exacts gifts tears it down.

5 A man who flatters his neighbor spreads a net for his feet.

6 An evil man is ensnared in his transgression, but a righteous man sings and rejoices.

7 A righteous man knows the rights of the poor; a wicked man does not understand such knowledge.

8 Scoffers set a city aflame**, but the wise turn away wrath.

9 If a wise man has an argument with a fool, the fool only rages and laughs, and there is no quiet.

10 Bloodthirsty*** men hate one who is blameless and seek the life of the upright.

---

* squander [skwɑ́ndər] ⑧ 낭비하다 ⑲ 낭비.

** aflame [əfléim] ⑲ 불타올라.

*** bloodthirsty [blə́dθə̀rsti] ⑲ 피에 굶주린, 잔인한.

11 A fool gives full vent* to his spirit, but a wise man quietly holds it back.

12 If a ruler listens to falsehood, all his officials will be wicked.

13 The poor man and the oppressor meet together; the LORD gives light to the eyes of both.

14 If a king faithfully judges the poor, his throne will be established forever.

15 The rod and reproof give wisdom, but a child left to himself brings shame to his mother.

16 When the wicked increase, transgression increases, but the righteous will look upon their downfall.

17 Discipline your son, and he will give you rest; he will give delight to your heart.

18 Where there is no prophetic** vision the people cast off restraint, but blessed is he who keeps the law.

19 By mere words a servant is not disciplined, for though he understands, he will not respond.

20 Do you see a man who is hasty in his words? There is more hope for a fool than for him.

---

* vent [vent] ⑧ 분출하다. 드러내다 ⑨ 배출구. 구멍.

** prophetic [prəfétik] ⑱ 묵시의. 예언자의. 예언의.

21 Whoever pampers* his servant from childhood will in the end find him his heir.

22 A man of wrath stirs up strife, and one given to anger causes much transgression.

23 One's pride will bring him low, but he who is lowly in spirit will obtain honor.

24 The partner of a thief hates his own life; he hears the curse, but discloses nothing.

25 The fear of man lays a snare, but whoever trusts in the LORD is safe.

26 Many seek the face of a ruler, but it is from the LORD that a man gets justice.

27 An unjust man is an abomination to the righteous, but one whose way is straight is an abomination to the wicked.

---

*   pamper [pǽmpər] ⑧ 애지중지하다. 버릇없이 키우다.

암송 구절 해설

**The fear of man lays a snare,
but whoever trusts in the LORD is safe(29:25).**

사람을 두려워하면 올무에 걸리게 되거니와
여호와를 의지하는 자는 안전하리라.

사람을 두려워하는 것은 다른 이들의 생각과 일을 염려하는 것이며, 하나님을 의지하는 것과 대립하는 행위입니다. 거기에는 올무가 도사리고 있습니다. 사람을 두려워하면 쉽사리 주님을 경외하지 못하고 위축이 되어 죄를 짓게 되기 때문입니다. 따라서 우리는 매사에 여호와를 신뢰하고, 인간의 힘과 견해는 주님께 견주었을 때 아무것도 아님을 인정하는 태도로 살아야 합니다. 주님을 의지하는 사람은 인간의 힘이 미치지 못하는 곳으로 높이 들려 죄에서 보호 받는다는 사실을 기억해야 합니다.

✏️ 하루 한 문장, 생각 쓰기   오늘 본문을 쓰면서 깨달은 지혜, 새롭게 다짐한 점,
떠오른 생각 등을 자유롭게 적어 보세요.

Proverbs 30

The Words of Agur

1 The words of Agur son of Jakeh. The oracle*. The man declares, I am weary, O God; I am weary, O God, and worn out.

2 Surely I am too stupid to be a man. I have not the understanding of a man.

3 I have not learned wisdom, nor have I knowledge of the Holy One.

4 Who has ascended to** heaven and come down? Who has gathered the wind in his fists? Who has wrapped up the waters in a garment? Who has established all the ends of the earth? What is his name, and what is his son's name? Surely you know!

5 Every word of God proves true; he is a shield to those who take refuge in him.

6 Do not add to his words, lest he rebuke you and you be found a liar.

7 Two things I ask of you; deny them not to me before I die:

8 Remove far from me falsehood and lying; give me neither poverty nor riches; feed me with the food that is needful for me,

9 lest I be full and deny you and say, "Who is the LORD?" or lest I be poor and steal and profane the name of my God.

10 Do not slander a servant to his master, lest he curse you, and you be held guilty.

11 There are those who curse their fathers and do not bless their mothers.

---

* oracle [ɔ́:rəkl] ⑲ 말씀. 신탁. 성경.

** ascend to ~로 올라가다.

12 There are those who are clean in their own eyes but are not washed of their filth.

13 There are those—how lofty are their eyes, how high their eyelids lift!

14 There are those whose teeth are swords, whose fangs* are knives, to devour the poor from off the earth, the needy from among mankind.

15 The leech** has two daughters: Give and Give. Three things are never satisfied; four never say, "Enough":

16 Sheol, the barren womb, the land never satisfied with water, and the fire that never says, "Enough."

17 The eye that mocks a father and scorns to obey a mother will be picked out by the ravens*** of the valley and eaten by the vultures.

18 Three things are too wonderful for me; four I do not understand:

19 the way of an eagle in the sky, the way of a serpent on a rock, the way of a ship on the high seas, and the way of a man with a virgin.

20 This is the way of an adulteress: she eats and wipes her mouth and says, "I have done no wrong."

21 Under three things the earth trembles; under four it cannot bear up:

22 a slave when he becomes king, and a fool when he is filled with food;

23 an unloved woman when she gets a husband, and a maidservant when she displaces her mistress.

---

*   fang [fæŋ] ⑲ 송곳니.
**   leech [liːtʃ] ⑲ 거머리. 고리대금업자.
*** raven [réivn] ⑲ 까마귀.

24 Four things on earth are small, but they are exceedingly wise:

25 the ants are a people not strong, yet they provide their food in the summer;

26 the rock badgers are a people not mighty, yet they make their homes in the cliffs;

27 the locusts* have no king, yet all of them march in rank;

28 the lizard you can take in your hands, yet it is in kings' palaces.

29 Three things are stately in their tread; four are stately in their stride:

30 the lion, which is mightiest among beasts and does not turn back before any;

31 the strutting** rooster, the he-goat, and a king whose army is with him.

32 If you have been foolish, exalting yourself, or if you have been devising evil, put your hand on your mouth.

33 For pressing milk produces curds, pressing the nose produces blood, and pressing anger produces strife.

---

*   locust [lóukəst] 명 메뚜기.
**   strutting [strʌtiŋ] 형 뽐내며 걷는, 위풍 있게 걷는.

암송 구절 해설

Every word of God proves true;
he is a shield to those who take refuge in him(30:5).

하나님의 말씀은 다 순전하며
하나님은 그를 의지하는 자의 방패시니라.

하나님의 말씀이 순전하다는 것은 모든 시험을 거쳤음을 의미합니다. 즉, 원석에서 불순물을 모두 제거하는 과정이 끝났기에 말씀이 순전하고 참되다는 것입니다. 진정한 방패는 자신의 명철을 의지하기보다는 주님을 온전히 신뢰하고(그분께로 피하고), 그분의 말씀을 마음에 새기는 이들에게만 찾아온다는 사실을 기억해야 합니다.

오늘 본문을 쓰면서 깨달은 지혜, 새롭게 다짐한 점,
떠오른 생각 등을 자유롭게 적어 보세요.

Proverbs 31

The Words of King Lemuel

1 The words of King Lemuel. An oracle that his mother taught him:

2 What are you doing, my son? What are you doing, son of my womb? What are you doing, son of my vows*?

3 Do not give your strength to women, your ways to those who destroy kings.

4 It is not for kings, O Lemuel, it is not for kings to drink wine, or for rulers to take strong drink,

5 lest they drink and forget what has been decreed and pervert the rights of all the afflicted.

6 Give strong drink to the one who is perishing, and wine to those in bitter distress;

7 let them drink and forget their poverty and remember their misery no more.

8 Open your mouth for the mute, for the rights of all who are destitute.

9 Open your mouth, judge righteously, defend the rights of the poor and needy.

The Woman Who Fears the Lord

10 An excellent wife who can find? She is far more precious than jewels.

---

*   VOW [vau] 몡 서원, 서약 통 맹세하다.

11 The heart of her husband trusts in her, and he will have no lack of gain.

12 She does him good, and not harm, all the days of her life.

13 She seeks wool and flax*, and works with willing hands.

14 She is like the ships of the merchant; she brings her food from afar**.

15 She rises while it is yet night and provides food for her household and portions for her maidens***.

16 She considers a field and buys it; with the fruit of her hands she plants a vineyard.

17 She dresses herself with strength and makes her arms strong.

18 She perceives that her merchandise is profitable. Her lamp does not go out at night.

19 She puts her hands to the distaff, and her hands hold the spindle.

20 She opens her hand to the poor and reaches out her hands to the needy.

21 She is not afraid of snow for her household, for all her household are clothed in scarlet.

22 She makes bed coverings for herself; her clothing is fine linen and purple.

23 Her husband is known in the gates when he sits among the elders of the land.

---

*   flax [flæks] ⑲ 아마포, 리넨.

**   afar [əfɑ́:r] ⑲ 멀리서.

*** maiden [méidn] ⑲ 처녀, 소녀, 아가씨.

24 She makes linen garments and sells them; she delivers sashes* to the merchant.

25 Strength and dignity** are her clothing, and she laughs at the time to come.

26 She opens her mouth with wisdom, and the teaching of kindness is on her tongue.

27 She looks well to the ways of her household and does not eat the bread of idleness.

28 Her children rise up and call her blessed; her husband also, and he praises her:

29 "Many women have done excellently, but you surpass them all."

30 Charm is deceitful, and beauty is vain, but a woman who fears the LORD is to be praised.

31 Give her of the fruit of her hands, and let her works praise her in the gates.

---

*   sash [sæʃ] ⑲ 띠.
** dignity [dígnəti] ⑲ 위엄. 존귀. 품격.

암송 구절 해설

An excellent wife who can find?
She is far more precious than jewels(31:10).

누가 현숙한 여인을 찾아 얻겠느냐
그의 값은 진주보다 더 하니라.

현숙한 여인은 힘과 용기를 지닌 여인 혹은 아내를 뜻합니다. 그녀는 능력이 출중하고 성격도 좋습니다. '누가 그런 여인을 찾아 얻겠느냐'는 질문은 그런 여인이 아주 드물어 진주보다 더 귀중함을 강조한 표현입니다. 즉, 그런 아내를 얻는 남자는 실로 희귀한 보배를 얻는 것이나 다름없습니다.

오늘 본문을 쓰면서 깨달은 지혜, 새롭게 다짐한 점.
떠오른 생각 등을 자유롭게 적어 보세요.

사랑을 더하면 온전해집니다.

이 모든 것 위에 사랑을 더하라 이는 온전하게 매는 띠니라(골 3:14).

도서출판 사랑플러스는 이 땅의 모든 교회와 성도들을 섬기기 위해 국제제자훈련원이 설립한 출판 사역 기관입니다.

십대를 위한 잠언 영어로 한 달 쓰기

초판 1쇄 인쇄 2020년 7월 1일
초판 1쇄 발행 2020년 7월 6일

엮은이 사랑플러스 편집부

펴낸이 오정현
펴낸곳 사랑플러스
등록번호 제2002-000032호(2002년 2월 15일)
주소 서울시 서초구 효령로 68길 98(서초동)
전화 02)3489-4300 **팩스** 02)3489-4329
이메일 dmipress@sarang.org

ISBN 979-11-88402-05-2 43230

※ 책값은 뒤표지에 있습니다. 잘못된 책은 구입하신 곳에서 교환해드립니다.

잠언 쓰기를 마치며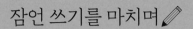

31일간 잠언을 쓰면서 깨달은 점 등을 기록해 보세요.

마친 날

년.　　　월.　　　일.